BRANCH LINES AROUND
1923 - 46
PORTMADOC

Vic Mitchell and Keith Smith

MP Middleton Press

Published to commemorate the 70th
anniversary of the union of the Welsh Highland
and Festiniog Railways in June 1923.

Cover picture: A boy scout in traditional uniform observes the activity at Portmadoc Harbour on 8th August 1935. Taliesin stands near the goods shed, discharging water and smoke before departing for Blaenau Ffestiniog, while Baldwin 4-6-0T no.590 makes up a train for the Welsh Highland route, only a year before its closure. (H.F.Wheeller/WHR)

First published April 1993
Reprinted March 1994

ISBN 1 873793 13 8

© *Middleton Press 1993*

Design - Deborah Goodridge
Typesetting - Barbara Mitchell

Published by Middleton Press
            Easebourne Lane
            Midhurst
            West Sussex
            GU29 9AZ
            Tel: (0730) 813169

Printed & bound by Biddles Ltd,
            Guildford and Kings Lynn

CONTENTS

Subsequent pages are not numbered to avoid intrusion into the illustrations. Photographs are numbered for precise identification instead.

INDEX

Portmadoc is lower centre on this map of 1923.
(Railway Magazine)

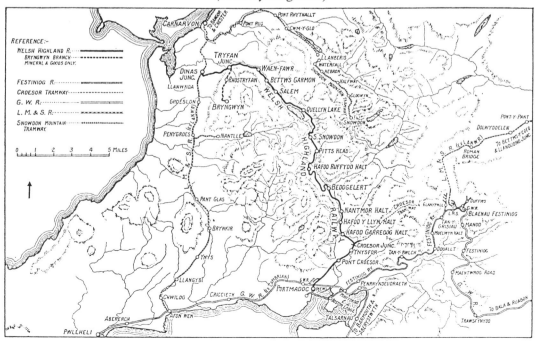

ACKNOWLEDGEMENTS

We are very grateful to so many who have helped with the compilation of this album. These include D.Allan and J.Keylock of the Welsh Highland Railway who have provided so many photographs of that line; M.Davies who has provided the traffic statistics; B.Cawkwell, K.Dakin, E.Goldsborough, D.Lusby, C.Morgan, Mr. D. & Dr. S.Salter, R.D.Smith, Mr & Mrs N.Stanyon who helped analyse them; G.Ive who computerised them and produced the graphs; and J.Miller and P.Shaw for access to the Colonel Stephens Railways Archive. We also appreciate the help received from Mrs. J.E.Baker, J.N.Faulkner (The Railway Club), Mrs E.A.Griffiths, P.Johnson, A.Ll.Lambert and Miss M. Wheeller.

Prints of the photographs marked WHR are available from that railway's shop at Porthmadog and those marked Lens of Sutton from 4 Westmead Road, Sutton, Surrey. Photographs attributed to C.Mowat are available from W.R.Burton, 3 Fairway, Clifton, York. Many of Colonel Stephens' archives can be seen at Tenterden Museum and some FR archives are on show in the museum in Harbour Station, Porthmadog.

PLACE NAMES

During the nineteenth century great efforts were made by outsiders to anglicise Wales, resulting in confusion in the spelling of place names. For historical accuracy and consistency, the form used by the railways in the period covered by this book is generally adopted, although it may differ from the Ordnance Survey.

The Festiniog Railway's Act of Parliament was passed with only one "F" and so the railway's name cannot easily be changed, although it is now marketed with two.

In giving a guide to pronunciation, it must be assumed that the reader has heard the unique Welsh sound of "ll". The places are listed in journey order.

Dinas	Deenas
Tryfan	Truvan
Waenfawr	Wine-vower
Bettws Garmon	Bettoos Garmon
Quellyn	Kwellin
Rhyd Ddu	Read Thee
Beddgelert	Beth-gelert (hard g)
Ynysfor	Un-is-vor
Minffordd	Mean-forth
Penrhyn	Pen-reen
Tanybwlch	Tan-er-boolk
Dduallt	Thee-allt
Tanygrisiau	Tan-er-grish-yah
Blaenau	Bly-nigh
Duffws	Dee-foos

HISTORICAL BACKGROUND

Festiniog Railway

An Act of Parliament was obtained in 1832 for the construction of the line which was intended to facilitate the conveyance of slates from the quarries of the Blaenau Ffestiniog district to the shipping wharfs at the then new town of Portmadoc. Gravity and horses were to be the main sources of power on the route, which was (six years after opening) on a continuous down gradient to the sea and nearly 14 miles in length.

Traffic commenced in 1836 and increased greatly, necessitating the replacement of the horses by steam locomotives in 1863 for hauling the empty slate wagons back to the quarries. Passenger traffic started officially in 1865.

The line prospered as a general carrier, double engines being introduced in 1869 to increase capacity. Blaenau Ffestiniog was reached by the London & North Western Railway in 1879 and by the Great Western Railway in 1882. By the end of the century, these factors, combined with a decreasing demand for slate, resulted in substantially reduced revenue for the FR.

The demands of World War I reduced the maintenance of the line and its ability to meet the competition of the emerging road transport industry after 1918. Despite the development of tourism between the wars and the hopes of expanding this traffic in association with the 1923 Welsh Highland Railway, the company's fortunes continued to decline.

WWII resulted in the cessation of passenger services on 15th September 1939 but slate trains continued until 1st August 1946. The line's subsequent revival will be the subject of another album in this series.

Welsh Highland Railway

Opening fully from Dinas Junction to Portmadoc on 8th June 1923, the WHR comprised three former concerns. From north to south, there was first the North Wales Narrow Gauge Railways which had been opened from Dinas Junction on the LNWR's 1872 Caernarvon-Afon Wen line. The NWNGR had begun passenger operation south to the west end of Quellyn Lake on 15th August 1877, was extended to the east end on 1st June 1878 and to Rhyd-Ddu (later South Snowdon) on 14th May 1881. Passenger services ceased on this line, and on its 1877 Bryngwyn branch, on 1st October 1916, the latter never to be restored. Goods traffic ran as required after 1916.

Secondly, under an Act of 1901, the Portmadoc, Beddgelert & South Snowdon Railway was incorporated, but the company achieved little, only the construction of a few earthworks and the ordering of *Russell* and six electric locomotives.

Thirdly, the horse-worked Croesor Tramway had operated north-eastwards from Portmadoc since 1863/4, carrying slates from the quarries of the Croesor Valley to the harbour.

The WHR was formed in 1922 and was empowered under a Light Railway Order to complete the railway from South Snowdon to Portmadoc New, a new station south of the Cambrian Coast line and it acquired the NWNGR and the PB&SSR.

Passenger openings were thus -

31 July 1922	Dinas Jn. - South Snowdon
1 June 1923	South Snowdon- Portmadoc New
8 June 1923	Portmadoc New - Harbour

The line was a financial disaster, went into receivership in March 1927, was leased by the FR from 1st July 1934 and saw its last passenger train on 26th September 1936. An occasional goods train ran until 19th June 1937, closure following on 1st July 1937.

The decisions concerning the lease of the WHR were astonishing. A trial period from July to October 1934 was agreed for a nominal £1 rental but the WHR returned a hefty £506 loss during the first six months. Despite this, the FR committed itself to a 42-year lease. The terms were that 10% of gross receipts would be paid until 1948; an additional 5% on receipts over £2000pa were due until 1955 when the figures would be reviewed. In 1935 there was a loss of £496 to which £100 had to be added, representing the 10% of receipts. A similar loss was recorded for 1936, this being offset by the meagre profit made by operating the FR.

On the last day of 1936, the FR told the Investing Authorities that "both railways had been given equal publicity. Our experience, however, has been that the WHR does not appeal to the public in anything like the same degree as does our own railway. The latter has a length of 13 miles and travels an appreciable part of its line through scenery which is not open to the tourist by any other means of transport. In addition its known antiquity and recent centenary are other factors contributing in no small degree to its popularity. The WHR on the other hand, with its long length of 22 miles, though passing by or through such well known beauty spots as the Pass of Aberglaslyn and Beddgelert, has nothing but its novelty to recommend it to the public. The two places last mentioned are equally accessible by road". The FR sought to be released from the lease but this was refused. A further attempt succeeded in 1942, as there was by then no longer a railway that could be run. All steel had been removed under a Defence Regulations Requisition Order, lifting commencing in August 1941.

The figures quoted are from the extensive archives of the companies and may not agree with those published previously.

1. The PB&SSR commenced the extension southwards from Beddgelert by constructing some embankments and overbridges. They were not used by the WHR, which was built further west, but this bridge remains over the A487 to this day and the abutments and wing walls of another stand in isolation in a field nearby. (R.Willliams/WHR)

KEY FIGURES

Personnel and finance are not usually considered in our albums but an exception is made here on account of two outstanding characters and the extraordinary matter of the lease.

Mr H.J.Jack was largely responsible for the formation of the WHR and was its chairman. He had no experience of public railways, having in earlier times been a wine merchant. Today he might be described as a "whizz kid" or entrepreneur. He was also chairman of the North Wales Power & Traction Company and envisaged supplying current to an electrified WHR. This hydro-electric business and another of his interests, the Aluminium Corporation, were based at Dolgarrog in the Conway Valley. He became a member of, and eventually chairman of, Caernarvonshire County Council and was able to introduce large sums of public money into the WHR from district, county and government sources (the latter ostensibly to relieve unemployment, but local labour "was found to be unsuitable"). At an acrimonious AGM of the WHR in November 1924, Jack was forced to resign as the appalling financial results were not in accordance with his optimistic expectations and much embarrassment was caused by the potential loss of public funds. (This became a reality). Henry Jack had also become chairman of the FR in 1921 and was, until 1922, receiver of the NWNGR and director of the PB&SSR! The locals had become suspicious. Jack resigned as chairman of the FR on 20th November 1924.

Lt Col H.F.Stephens had acquired a reputation for the engineering, construction and management of minor railways in various parts of Britain. Prior to WWI, Holman Stephens controlled or influenced a number of successful lines but their deterioration following the advent of effective road transport resulted in a collection of ramshackle railways with unorthodox equipment and methods of operation. (Some are illustrated in four companion Middleton Press albums - *Branch Line to Selsey, Shrewsbury, Tenterden and East Kent Light Railway*).

The Colonel was appointed civil engineer and locomotive superintendent to both the FR and the WHR on 1st April 1923. Thus two more railways were added to the nameboard

Continued →

GEOGRAPHICAL SETTING

The WHR's northern terminus was on the rising coastal plain, three miles south of the county town of Caernarvon. The route ran eastwards to Waenfawr, where it entered the valley of the north flowing Afon Gwyrfai, which it followed closely to Rhyd-Ddu. The river widens to form a mile-long lake, Llyn Quellyn, north of Rhyd-Ddu where the station was renamed, inaccurately, South Snowdon, being on the *west* flank of the mountain.

Iron and non-ferrous metals had been mined in the valley, but not during the life of the WHR. Production of slates (of an inferior quality) was in decline when the WHR opened and only small quantities were carried.

The summit of the line (650ft above sea level) was near Pitt's Head, almost a mile south of South Snowdon. The track descended steeply, often at 1 in 40, round numerous sharp curves which followed the contours of the steep sided valley of the Afon Colwyn to reach Beddgelert. The village is at the confluence of the Colwyn and Glaslyn, the latter flowing south through the narrow Pass of Aberglaslyn to eventually enter the sea at Portmadoc.

South of Nantmor, the track descended onto the flat ground reclaimed from the sea, following the completion of Madock's embankment south-east of Portmadoc.

The population of the district served by the WHR is of interest, as it alone would not have justified a railway, particularly one that did not reach Caernarvon.

	1921	1931
Waenfawr	1280	1260
Bettws Garmon & Rhyd-Dhu	340	327
Beddgelert & Nantmor	1055	913
Llanfrothen & Croesor	713	653
Note the universal decline during the decade.	3380	3153

Portmadoc and its harbour were established in the 1820s, as the construction of the embankment or Cob resulted in the Afon Glaslyn scouring a deep channel near the tidal sluices. The port was suitable for the ships of the period and the town expanded as a result of the increasing trade, being laid out in a symmetrical pattern, as was common in new towns.

The FR terminus is at the Harbour and its first mile traverses the level Cob. Thereafter the line was designed to be on a continuous rising gradient. To Penrhyndeudraeth the route is along a tapering finger of high ground that separates the valleys of the Glaslyn and the Dwyryd, the latter river being the main feature of the Vale of Ffestiniog. By Dduallt, the line is over 500ft above the valley floor and passes through part of the Moelwyn mountain range by means of a tunnel. In this vicinity granite was of economic importance, but the predominant mineral worked from here northwards is slate of high quality.

From Tanygrisiau the route runs up the valley of the Afon Barlwyd. It is in the urban area of Blaenau Ffestiniog for its final mile, being overshadowed by mountains and slate rubbish tips. The town is one of the highest in Wales at over 700ft above sea level.

Unless otherwise stated, the maps are to the scale of 25" to 1 mile and are from the 1914-19 edition of the Ordnance Survey. That organisation made no survey during the period covered by this book and so the section between Beddgelert and Croesor Junction was not recorded officially.

on the exterior of his office at Tonbridge in Kent, which was involved over the years with no less than 17 railways. The organisation of the two Welsh lines was thus unsatisfactorily split between five offices - Dolgarrog, Tonbridge, Dinas Junction, Portmadoc Harbour and Buckingham Gate, London SW1, the FR Company's registered office. Stephens became chairman and managing director of the FR on 1st January 1925.

Much of the correspondence between Portmadoc and Tonbridge survives. Southbound were lengthy explanations for late running and northbound were curt, brief often sarcastic comments from a military man who developed a great antagonism with local staff. Some extracts are included in this volume. Stephens died in 1931 but some of the administrative work continued to be done in Kent up to the closure of both lines.

LOCOMOTIVES

Welsh Highland Railway

Moel Tryfan was the only one of three single Fairlie articulated 0-6-4Ts supplied to the NWNGR to enter WHR stock. It was built by the Vulcan Foundry in 1875 and cut up in 1954 on the FR.

Russell was the only other engine to work on the NWNGR and to continue to work the line when the WHR was formed. A substantial 2-6-2T, it was built by Hunslet in 1906 and remained at Dinas Junction after the line closed. After two spells in industry and a long time as a museum exhibit, the engine returned to the present WHR in 1977.

No.590 was built in the USA by Baldwin Locomotive Works in 1917 for use in France during WWI. Colonel Stephens arranged its purchase and it arrived on the WHR in July 1923 but it was not very successful. It survived the WHR closure but was too large to work on the FR. It was broken up in 1942 at Dinas Junction.

Jack ordered that *Moel Tryfan* and *Russell* be cut down to fit the FR loading gauge. The former ran successfully to Blaenau Ffestiniog (in 1924 only) but the latter is reputed to have jammed in Moelwyn Tunnel and was thus restricted to the WHR.

Festiniog Railway

Prince, Princess, Palmerston, Welsh Pony and *Little Giant* were all built by George England & Company in South London in 1863-67 and were all still on the FR in the 1930s. (All but the last named exist today). Being 0-4-0s, their adhesive weight was limited and the double engine design was soon adopted.

There were three 0-4-4-0 Fairlies in use during the period of this book - *James Spooner* (dismantled 1933), *Merddin Emrys* and *Livingston Thompson* (renamed Taliesin in 1932 and Earl of Merioneth in 1961). The first *Taliesin* was a single Fairlie 0-4-4T, built in 1876 and withdrawn in 1930.

PASSENGER COACHES

Welsh Highland Railway

By 1922 the NWNGR stock was fairly rotten after years of disuse and neglect. Of the 20 vehicles in store, eleven were repaired and repainted. These were mostly bogie coaches and included four built by Ashbury in 1894 as "summer coaches" with half-height doors (one is now FR no.26), a Cleminson six-wheeler from the Gloucester Wagon Co. and two provided by Pickering & Co. in 1907. To these were added in 1923 six open-sided "toastrack" cars from Robert Hudson, each seating 30 people. They were paid for by the FR and probably used on both systems but were short-lived.

Festiniog Railway

The original 1865 fleet of diminutive four-wheelers with longitudinal seating was largely usable in the period under consideration. To this had been added a much larger stock of four-wheelers for use by quarrymen but, having very few windows, they were unsuitable for tourists. The 1865 coaches were built by Brown, Marshalls & Co of Birmingham, as were the first two bogie coaches which followed in 1872. Not only were they the first on the FR but the first in Britain in regular service (Nos. 15 and 16 survive today). Two more followed in 1876 from the same builder and a further two from Gloucester in 1879. Five bogie vans were added to the fleet, of which three were rebuilt with some passenger compartments in the 1920s, nos. 10-12 being the survivors today.

PORTMADOC (Harbour) and BLAENAU FESTINIOG.—Festiniog			July 1937						
Miles	Down	Week Days only			Miles	Up	Week Days only		
		mrn mrn aft aft aft					mrn aft	aft	aft
—	Portmadoc (Harbour) dep.	5 20 10 15 12 20 3 10 5 55	..		—	Blaenau { G.W. dep 11 32 1 35	..	1 23	7 7	..
1	Boston Lodge Halt **A**	..	..			Festiniog { L.M.S. 11 35 1 40	..	4 26	7 10	..
2	Minffordd 146	5 30 10 30 12 30 3 20 6 8	..		1½	Tanygrisiau 11 40 1 45	..	4 31	7A15	..
3½	Penrhyndeudraeth 147	5 35 10 35 12 35 3 28 6 13	..		2½	Moelwyn Halt	..	Aa	..
7	Tanybwlch, for Maentwrog	5 55 10 55 12 55 3 48 6 33	..		3½	Dduallt Aa Aa	..	Aa	..
9½	Dduallt	Aa	Aa	..		5½	Tanybwlch, for Maentwrog 12 02	..	4 50	7 33	..
10½	Moelwyn Halt	Aa	..		9	Penrhyndeudraeth 147 12 20 2 25	..	5 10	7A53	..
11	Tanygrisiau	6 15	..		10½	Minffordd 146 12 29 2 33	..	5 18	7 53	..
12½	Blaenau Fest. { L.M.S.	6 29 11 29 1 29 4 13 6 58	..		11	Boston Lodge Halt **A**	..	8	..
12½	iniog 148, 565 { G.W. arr.	6 33 11 33 1 33 4 17 7 0	..		12½	Portmadoc (Har.) 146 arr. 12 38 2 42	..	5 27	8 9	..
		A For Portmeirion and Gwyllt Flower Gardens					**A** or **Aa** Stops if required		

PASSENGER SERVICES

The table is intended to give an indication of the trends, the summer columns showing the peak period frequency and the winter columns give the minimum service or that operating in the early months of the year concerned.

As the ticket sales graphs show, the FR carried a few ordinary passengers on the quarryman's trains each winter throughout the 1930s. These trains were not advertised in the public timetables and so are not included in the table opposite.

It is interesting to note that the number of trains run on the WHR some winter months exceeded the number of tickets issued in the entire month. When examining the figures and graphs, the effect of two major strikes will be seen. The general strike throughout Britain was 4th May to 13th July 1926 and a strike in the quarries lasted from 14th March to 16th May 1936.

	FR		WHR	
	WINTER	SUMMER	WINTER	SUMMER
1923	6	8	-	6
1924	5	9	3	6a
1925	5	5	1	3a
1926	5	5	1	2a
1927	5	6	1c	3ab
1928	4	7	1c	1bb
1929	4	5	1c	1
1930	1	3	-	1c
1931	-	3	-	1
1932	-	3	-	1
1933	-	5	-	1
1934	-	6	-	3
1935	-	4	-	3
1936	-	5	-	3
1937	-	5	-	-
1938	-	4	-	-
1939	-	5	-	-

a = One extra south of Beddgelert
b = One extra south of South Snowdon
c = North of Beddgelert only and on Mondays, Wednesdays and Fridays only

DINAS JUNCTION, PORTMADOC, BLAENAU FESTINIOG, and DUFFWS.—Welsh Highland and Festiniog. August 1926

Week Days only.

Miles		mrn	mrn	mrn	aft	aft	aft
	Dinas Junction ....dep.					1255	4 40
2	Tryfan Junction					1 8	4 53
3¾	Waenfawr					1 22	5 5
4½	Bettws Garmon					1 27	5 10
5½	Salem					Aa	Aa
—	Plas-y-Nant					Aa	Aa
7¼	Quellyn Lake					1 44	5 27
9¼	South Snowdon A ... arr.					1 52	5 35
	dep.					2 0	5 38
10¼	Pitt's Head					Aa	Aa
11¼	Hafod Ruffydd					Aa	Aa
13¼	Beddgelert .... arr.					2 25	6 3
	dep.				12 20	3 0	6 10
15¼	Nantmor, for Aberglaslyn				12A33	3A12	6 22
16¼	Hafod-y-Llyn				Aa	Aa	Aa
17¼	Hafod Garregog				Aa	Aa	Aa
18¼	Ynysfor, for Llanfrothen				12 47	3 28	6 38
19¼	Pont Croesor, for Prenteg				12 53	3 34	6 44
21¼	Portmadoc (N.) B 140 arr.				1 5	3 46	6 56
	dep.				1 7	3 48	
—	" (Old)	5 15	7 50	11 5	2 30	5 10	
24	Minffordd 140	5 26	8 2	1122	2 43	5 27	
25¼	Penrhyndeudraeth 141	5 33	8 9	1129	2 50	5 34	
29¼	Tanybwlch, for Maentwrog	5 57	8 33	1153	3 14	5 58	
31¼	Dduallt	Aa	Aa		Aa	Aa	
33¼	Tanygrisiau	6 19	8 56	1215	3 36	6 20	
34¼	Blaenau Festiniog 144, 504 L. M. S.	6 25	9 2	1221	3 42	6 26	
34¾	G. W.	6 27	9 4	1223	3 44	6 28	
35	Duffws ....arr.	6 28	9 5	1224	3 45	6 29	

Miles		mrn	mrn	aft (Saturdays only. Workmen's Train.)	aft	aft	aft	aft
	Duffws ....dep.	9 17		1225	1255		4 25	6 57
¼	Blaenau Festiniog G. W.	9 18		1226	1256		4 26	6 58
½	L. M. S.	9 20		1228	1257		4 28	7 3
1¼	Tanygrisiau	9 27		1235	1 4		4 35	7 9
3¼	Dduallt			Aa	Aa		Aa	
5¼	Tanybwlch, for Maentwrog	9 48		1256	1 26		4 57	7 29
9½	Penrhyndeudraeth 141	1010		1 16	1 47		5 18	7 50
11	Minffordd 140	1018		1 23	1 54		5 25	7 56
—	Portmadoc (Old) 140	1028	10 30	1 33	2 10	5 10	5 35	8 6
13¾	" (New) B .. arr.		10 34		2 12	5 14		
	dep.		11 20		2 14	5 16		
15¾	Pont Croesor, for Prenteg		11A35		2A23	5 25		
16¾	Ynysfor, for Llanfrothen		11A40		2A28	5 30		
17¾	Hafod Garregog		Aa		Aa	Aa		
18¾	Hafod-y-Llyn		Aa		Aa	Aa		
19¼	Nantmor, for Aberglaslyn		11 59		2 46	5 49		
21¾	Beddgelert .... arr.		12 11		2 58	6 1		
	dep.				3 1	6 5		
23¾	Hafod Ruffydd				Aa	Aa		
24¾	Pitt's Head				Aa	Aa		
25¾	South Snowdon A ... arr.				3 31	6 35		
	dep.				3 34	6 38		
27¾	Quellyn Lake				3 47	6 51		
—	Plas-y-Nant				Aa	Aa		
29¼	Salem				Aa	Aa		
30¼	Bettws Garmon				3 58	7 3		
31¼	Waenfawr				4 6	7 11		
33	Tryfan Junction				4 16	7 21		
35	Dinas Junction 514 ....arr.				4 25	7 30		

A About 3 miles to the Summit of Snowdon. A or Aa Stop when required. B Station for Borthygest; ½ mile to the G. W. Station.

DINAS JUNCTION, PORTMADOC, BLAENAU FESTINIOG, and DUFFWS.—Festiniog and Welsh Highland. July 1929

Week Days only.

Miles		mrn	mrn	mrn	aft	aft (Except Saturdays.)	aft
	Dinas Junction ....dep.					12 22	
2	Tryfan Junction					12 35	
3¾	Waenfawr					12 47	
4½	Bettws Garmon					12 52	
5½	Salem					Aa	
6	Plas-y-Nant					Aa	
7¼	Quellyn Lake					1 7	
9¼	South Snowdon A ... arr.					1 15	
	dep.					1 18	
10¼	Pitt's Head					Aa	
11¼	Hafod Ruffydd					Aa	
13¼	Beddgelert .... arr.					1 44	
	dep.					1 49	
15¼	Nantmor, for Aberglaslyn					1 58	
16¼	Hafod-y-Llyn					Aa	
17¼	Hafod Garregoz					Aa	
18	Croesor Junction					Aa	
18¼	Ynysfor, for Llanfrothen					2 14	
19¼	Pont Croesor, for Prenteg					2 19	
21¼	Portmadoc (N.) B 140 arr.					2 22	
	dep						3 0
21¾	" (Old)	5 15	7 55	10 56	2 20		3N9
22¼	Boston Lodge Halt	Aa	Aa	Aa	Aa		Aa
24	Minffordd 140	5 26	8 7	11K11	2 32		3L23
25¼	Penrhyndeudraeth 141	5A31	8A12	11A16	2A37		3A28
29¼	Tanybwlch, for Maentwrog	5 54	8 35	11 39	3 0		3 50
31¼	Dduallt	Aa	Aa	Aa	Aa		Aa
33¼	Tanygrisiau	6A14	8A55	11A59	3A20		4A10
34¼	Blaenau Festiniog 144, 504 L. M. S.	6 19	9 0	12 4	3 25		4 15
34¾	G. W.	6 22	9 2	12 6	3 27		4 17
35	Duffws ....arr.	6 23	9 3	12 7	3 28		4 18

Miles		mrn	mrn	aft (Except Saturdays.)	aft	aft	aft
	Duffws ....dep.	6 31	9 20	12 13		4 25	5 4
¼	Blaenau Festiniog G. W.	Aa	9 21	12 14		4 26	5 5
½	L. M. S.	Aa	9 23	12 16		4 28	5 7
1¼	Tanygrisiau	Aa	9A28	12A21		4A33	5A12
3¼	Dduallt	Aa	Aa	Aa		Aa	Aa
5¼	Tanybwlch, for Maentwrog	Aa	9 48	12 41		4 53	5 32
9½	Penrhyndeudraeth 141	Aa	1010A	1A2		5A15	5A53
11	Minffordd 140	Aa	1018	1 10		5 22	6 0
12	Boston Lodge Halt	Aa	Aa	Aa		Aa	Aa
13	Portmadoc (Old) 140	7 38	1028	1L24		5 32	6 10
13¾	" (New) B .. arr.			1 28			
	dep.				2 38		
15¾	Pont Croesor, for Prenteg				2A47		
16¾	Ynysfor, for Llanfrothen				2A52		
17	Croesor Junction				Aa		
17¾	Hafod Garregog				Aa		
18¾	Hafod-y-Llyn				Aa		
19¼	Nantmor, for Aberglaslyn				3A10		
21¾	Beddgelert .... arr.				3 22		
	dep.				4 45		
23¾	Hafod Ruffydd				Aa		
24¾	Pitt's Head				Aa		
25¾	South Snowdon A ... arr.				5 14		
	dep.				5 26		
27¾	Quellyn Lake				5A31		
28½	Plas-y-Nant				Aa		
29¼	Salem				Aa		
30¼	Bettws Garmon				5A43		
31¼	Waenfawr				5 51		
33	Tryfan Junction				6 1		
35	Dinas Junction 514 ....arr.				6 10		

A About 3 miles to the summit of Snowdon. A or Aa Stop when required. B Station for Borthygest; ½ mile to the G.W. Station. K Arrives at 11 6 mrn.
L Arrives 4 minutes *earlier*. N Arrives at 3 4 aft.
☞ Trains between Portmadoc and Blaenau Festiniog will depart from and arrive at **Portmadoc High Street Halt** on the Town side of Britannia Bridge.

TRAFFIC STATISTICS

The graphs have vertical lines representing each month with a space between each year. The figures are for tickets issued, not passengers journeys as now commonly quoted. The ratio of single to return tickets ranged from 1:1.6 to 1:2.1.

The vertical scales are not the same for each station so that direct visual comparisons should not be made.

FR Ordinary ticket totals

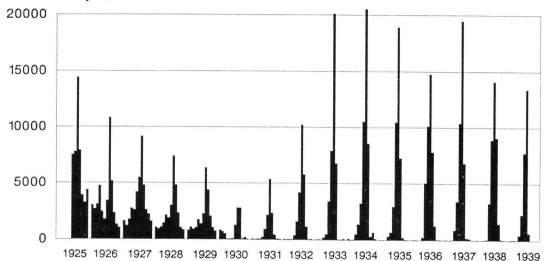

FR Workmans ticket totals

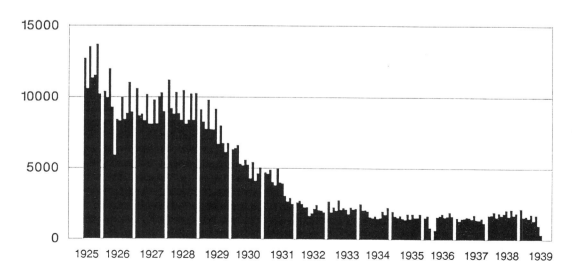

Comparison of FR workmans tickets and slate tonnage output of Bleanau Ffestiniog

Comparison of FR workmans tickets with total slate tonnage from the Blaenau Ffestiniog district reveals the point at which there was a substantial transfer to road transport.

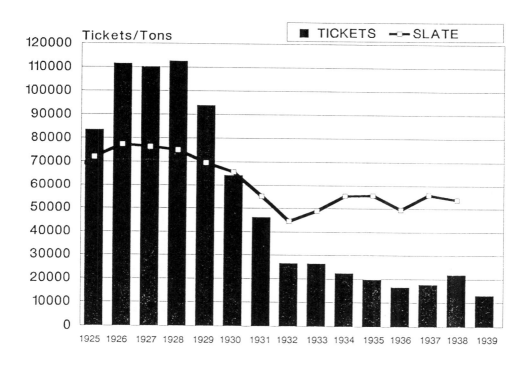

Transfer tickets from GWR to WHR

	1925	1926	1927	1928	1929	1930	1931	1932	1933	1934	1935	1936
January		0	0	0	0	0	0	0	0	0	0	0
February		0	0	0	0	0	0	0	0	0	0	0
March		0	0	0	0	0	0	0	0	0	0	0
April		0	0	0	0	0	0	0	0	0	0	0
May		0	0	0	0	0	0	0	0	0	0	0
June	102	0	38	0	0	0	0	0	0	0	0	0
July	244	70	212	36	0	0	0	0	0	51	101	120
August	524	775	827	65	14	0	0	19	0	212	305	254
September	444	271	218	682	44	0	0	4	0	101	227	128
October	0	12	0	49	59	0	0	0	0	0	0	0
November	0	0	0	0	0	0	0	0	0	0	0	0
December	0	0	0	0	0	0	0	0	0	0	0	0

Traffic returns were often made one or two months late

Transfer tickets from LMS to WHR

	1925	1926	1927	1928	1929	1930	1931	1932	1933	1934	1935	1936
January		28	3	0	0	0	0	0	0	0	0	0
February		0	0	0	0	0	0	0	0	0	0	0
March		11	0	0	0	0	0	0	0	0	0	0
April		21	6	0	0	1	0	0	0	0	0	0
May		0	39	0	2	0	0	0	0	0	0	0
June	600	0	278	72	73	18	0	0	0	0	0	0
July	1155	171	694	234	271	126	180	101	150	157	180	289
August	1770	1685	1330	540	835	291	471	317	520	623	431	1001
September	1085	571	401	1475	1477	171	254	1210	252	282	244	557
October	117	66	50	339	567	0	12	0	0	0	0	0
November	2	7	0	13	0	0	0	0	0	0	0	0
December	2	0	0	0	0	0	0	0	0	0	0	0

Traffic returns were often made one or two months late

Transfer tickets from FR to WHR

	1925	1926	1927	1928	1929	1930	1931	1932	1933	1934	1935	1936
January	1	0	0	0	0	0	0	0	0	0	0	0
February	1	0	0	0	0	0	0	0	0	0	0	0
March	0	1	0	0	0	0	0	0	0	0	0	0
April	14	7	0	0	0	0	0	0	0	0	0	0
May	0	3	11	0	17	0	0	0	0	0	0	0
June	46	4	60	0	20	46	0	0	0	0	0	0
July	87	28	82	52	18	0	18	62	206	653	821	1150
August	234	90	280	76	112	29	225	510	1271	1705	1488	1233
September	134	74	99	70	59	0	142	152	725	834	645	452
October	9	0	4	2	2	0	4	0	0	0	0	0
November	3	0	0	0	0	0	0	0	0	0	0	0
December	0	0	0	0	0	0	0	0	0	0	0	0

Transfer tickets from WHR to FR

	1925	1926	1927	1928	1929	1930	1931	1932	1933	1934	1935	1936
January	0	0	0	0	0	0	0	0	0	0	0	
February	0	0	0	0	0	0	0	0	0	0	0	
March	0	0	0	0	0	0	0	0	0	0	0	
April	0	0	0	0	0	0	0	0	0	0	0	
May	0	2	0	4	0	0	0	0	0	0	0	
June	13	0	19	0	34	0	0	0	0	0	0	
July	29	1	15	45	64	0	0	14	63	279	180	192
August	84	26	45	47	33	0	30	93	191	435	368	353
September	40	4	39	37	40	0	21	17	87	169	131	98
October	5	0	1	0	0	0	0	0	0	7	0	0
November	0	0	0	0	0	0	0	0	0	0	0	0
December	0	0	0	0	0	0	0	0	0	0	0	0

Transfer tickets from GWR to FR

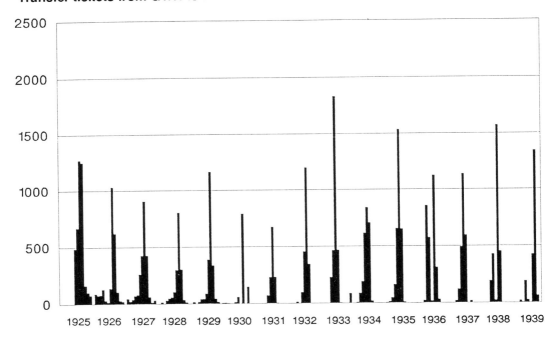

Transfer tickets from LMS to FR

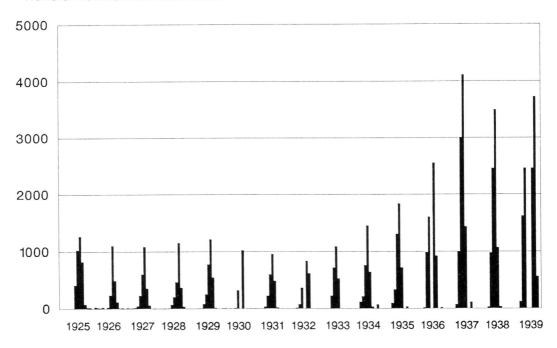

```
┌─────────────────────────────────────────────────────────────────────┐
```
Freight originating on the FR (tons)

	1920	1921	1930	1931	1933	1934
Flour, bran etc.	672	772	118	131	118	131
Grain	28	5	37	11		
Iron and steel bars, joists and plates	68	26	20	13	11	16
Iron and steel scrap	191	35	80	49	60	31
Iron and steel, other descriptions	268	189	57	52	39	33
Stone for roadmaking	15786	10860	15317	15165	8	309
Manure	17	14				
Potatoes	63	88	14	7		
Sand	230	262	125	185		
Slates, common	53204	53241	58824	50261	50661	54101
Timber, pitwood and mining	190	80	94	43		
Timber, other descriptions	374	330	12	8		
Oils, not dangerous					78	108

Horses, cattle, calves, sheep, pigs, miscellaneous live stock were nil for all years listed.

WHR ticket totals

	1925	1926	1927	1928	1929	1930	1931	1932	1933	1934	1935	1936
January		468	154	124	0	11	0	0	0	0	0	0
February		356	180	103	0	2	0	0	0	0	0	0
March		439	363	104	2	2	0	0	0	0	0	0
April		878	303	77	4	1	0	0	0	0	0	0
May		59	652	154	70	8	0	0	0	0	0	0
June	3492	0	1210	529	203	135	0	282	170	0	0	0
July	4604	1195	2450	894	608	309	357	340	949	2316	2187	3501
August	8335	6056	5033	2272	1574	603	1428	3036	4555	8360	7532	6113
September	4849	2645	2214	2619	1988	528	653	669	2153	3462	2925	2368
October	1011	377	235	513	632	0	25	0	0	0	0	0
November	652	220	73	15	2	0	0	0	0	0	0	0
December	431	209	150	1	3	0	0	0	0	0	0	0
Totals		12902	13017	7405	5086	1599	2463	4327	7827	14138	12644	11982

These figures include tickets issued by the GWR, LMS and FR for through journeys but exclude tickets sold at Portmadoc New in 1929-33, as no returns were made in that period.

WHR freight tonnage 1936-37

	SOUTH SNOWDON			BEDDGELERT		
	GOODS OUT	GOODS IN	COAL IN	GOODS OUT	GOODS IN	COAL IN
1936						
October	-	-	9	-	2	57
November	-	-	-	1	2	43
December	-	1	9	1	3	55
1937						
January	-	-	-	1	4	35
February	-	-	17	1	3	22
March	-	-	-	-	4	46
April	-	-	8	-	4	36
May	-	-	-	1	39	11
June	-	-	-	-	1	18

These tonnage returns for the final nine months of the WHR show the line in terminal decline. The mineral traffic had ceased apart from 169 tons *loaded* at Portmadoc in June 1936. Its destination was not shown. The last passengers had been carried in September 1936 - officially!

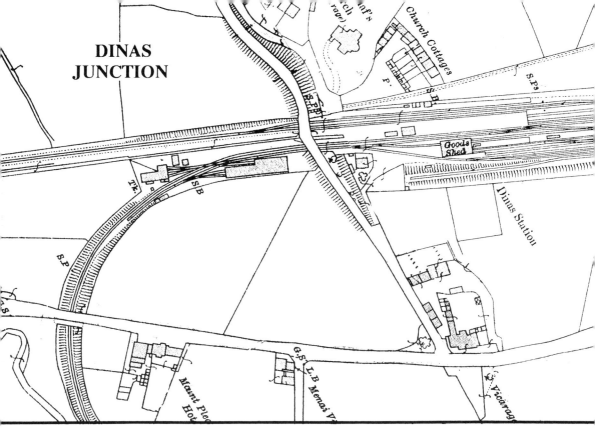

DINAS JUNCTION

2. On the left of this 1934 view are the two platforms of the former LNWR, which had become part of the London, Midland & Scottish Railway in 1923. The goods shed (right) had a narrow gauge siding passing through it and a standard gauge siding entering at the far end and terminating inside. The passenger access slope is lower left. (F.M.Gates/WHR)

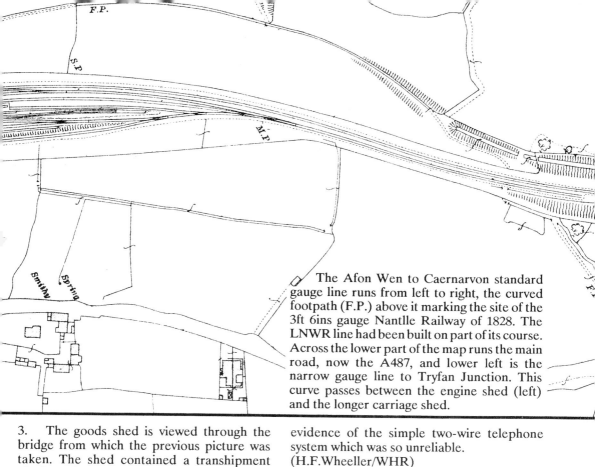

The Afon Wen to Caernarvon standard gauge line runs from left to right, the curved footpath (F.P.) above it marking the site of the 3ft 6ins gauge Nantlle Railway of 1828. The LNWR line had been built on part of its course. Across the lower part of the map runs the main road, now the A487, and lower left is the narrow gauge line to Tryfan Junction. This curve passes between the engine shed (left) and the longer carriage shed.

3. The goods shed is viewed through the bridge from which the previous picture was taken. The shed contained a transhipment platform between the two tracks. There is evidence of the simple two-wire telephone system which was so unreliable. (H.F.Wheeller/WHR)

4. Two partially glazed coaches are evident as a family waits on the grass covered platform, the sign behind them proclaiming DINAS JUNCTION CHANGE FOR SNOWDON BEDDGELERT PORTMADOC & BLAENAU FFESTINIOG. In the background is the station master's house, the cost of staffing and other expenses of the station being shared equally by the LMS and WHR until 1935. (Lens of Sutton)

5. At the north end of the site and in the background of picture no.2 were the slate transhipment wharves. Breakages were common; evidence is on the ground. On the other side of the yard, a tippler for standard gauge wagons facilitated transfer of coal to narrow gauge. (LGRP)

6. A view south from the road bridge includes (from left to right) the carriage shed, the curving main line, the engine shed, the signal box and the LMS line to Afon Wen. In 1992, the former railway sites were occupied by depots of the National Rivers Authority and Gwynedd County Council. Since 1916, the signal box had served only as a store. (F.M.Gates/WHR)

7. In line with the spire of the chapel is the water tank and to the right of it is the sand drying shed. To the right of the two-road engine shed is a lean-to workshop, reported as poorly equipped and devoid of machine tools. The scene was recorded in 1939 by which time grass was growing over the rails but the ash heap was still visible. (RAS Marketing/WHR)

8. Seen inside the shed in August 1938 is *Russell* (centre) and no.590. Latterly, this had been a running shed, repairs being undertaken at the FR's Boston Lodge Works. The adjacent workshop had earlier housed a lathe and drill. One of the side tanks off no.590 still exists today having been used for oil storage for nearly 50 years after the locomotive's demise in 1942. (D.W.K.Jones/Robert Humm)

Dinas Junction tickets issued

	1925	1926	1927	1928	1929	1930	1931	1932	1933	1934	1935	1936
January		47	145	9	0	11	0	0	0	0	0	0
February		33	166	5	0	2	0	0	0	0	0	0
March		53	177	4	2	2	0	0	0	0	0	0
April		161	25	15	4	0	0	0	0	0	0	0
May		14	246	52	51	8	0	0	0	0	0	0
June	841	0	175	315	110	71	0	282	170	0	0	0
July	855	209	311	171	319	183	159	177	593	837	1086	857
August	1478	783	479	305	613	283	732	2190	2744	2909	2515	2251
September	955	487	272	196	408	96	257	392	1176	1189	1021	671
October	133	252	131	23	4	0	9	0	0	0	0	0
November	74	199	20	2	2	0	0	0	0	0	0	0
December	54	205	10	1	3	0	0	0	0	0	0	0

9. From left to right is the white roofed tea room (once operated by the Snowdon Mountain Tramroad & Hotels Co. with which Jack was connected), the massive goods shed, the platform buildings, the station master's house, the road to Saron, the carriage shed and the engine shed. Photographed in 1942, the coaches had been drawn out into the open to be auctioned in June of that year. The WHR curves eastwards at the top of the picture.
(A.E.Rimmer/WHR coll.)

EAST OF DINAS JUNCTION

10. The route climbed through meadows and woodland mainly on a gradient of 1 in 47, with one section at 1 in 37. *Russell* would have needed plenty of dry sand here on damp days or when weeds lay on the rails. (WHR coll.)

TRYFAN JUNCTION

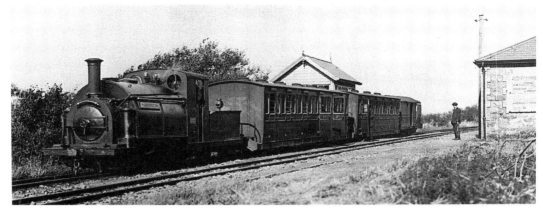

11. *Palmerston* waits with a train of FR coaches bound for Dinas Junction. The partially obscured signal box had 20 levers and once controlled no fewer than 10 signals. By 1927 none was working, and the branch was operated on the "One engine in steam" principle. The guard is holding a staff, which was kept in the telephone room of the unmanned station. A wooden staff was used to South Snowdon and a Wise's staff to Dinas Junction, together with written tickets when necessary. (P.Johnson coll/WHR)

The Dinas Junction - Waenfawr line runs from left to right and the Bryngwyn branch curves south at 3¾ chains radius on a 1 in 39 up gradient, a challenge to drivers especially in wet weather. The two road bridges and the station building were still standing in 1992, albeit the latter in extremely poor condition. In WHR days the loop was not used by passenger trains, only by trains from the branch.

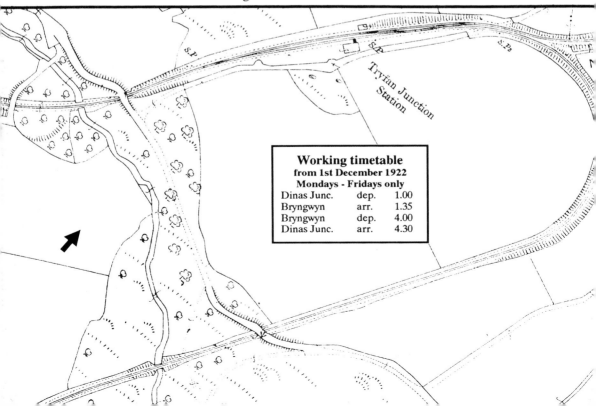

Working timetable
from 1st December 1922
Mondays - Fridays only

Dinas Junc.	dep.	1.00
Bryngwyn	arr.	1.35
Bryngwyn	dep.	4.00
Dinas Junc.	arr.	4.30

12. The nameboard was still in place when the station was photographed in 1941, four years after the last passenger passed this way. The station was demoted to a halt in 1934, having ceased to be a junction for passengers in 1916. (J.F.Bolton/WHR)

The branch carried much more slate traffic than the main line to the south, seeing four or five trains per week. After the closure of the Moel Tryfan Quarry in February 1935 there was only one goods train per week to Bryngwyn. In 1934 there had been an average of only 22 tons per week. The branch is shown at 1½" to 1 mile on the 1898 survey.

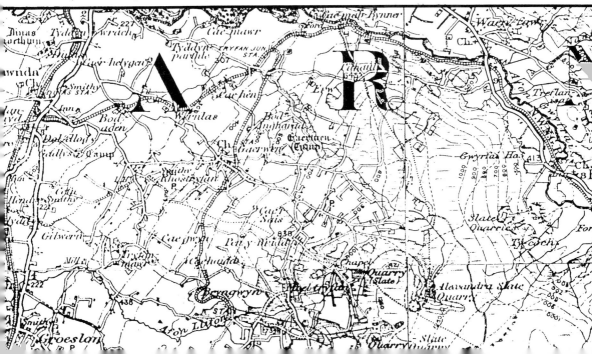

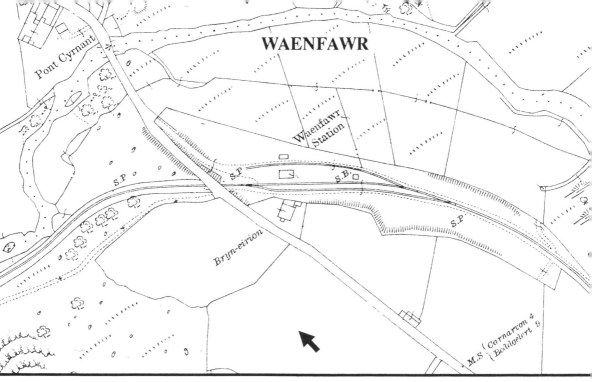

WAENFAWR

From Tryfan Junction the route was gently graded, and ran close to the river (marked with dots in mid-stream) on the valley floor. Bryn-eirion has become the Snowdonia Park Hotel.

13. A 1923 eastward view includes the then redundant signal box. The train is the same one which was recorded in picture no.11. In 1926, a siding to the Dudley Park Granite Quarry was opened. It ran south-westwards from the south end of the loop. (LGRP/WHR)

14. A later, but damaged, picture includes the shed, the purpose of which has not been recorded. Goods, coal and/or permanent way materials are items likely to have been stored therein. By 1992 the shed had gone, and the main building was a roofless ruin. (C.Mowat)

15. This postcard was endorsed *A Welsh Highland train, Beddgelert.* In fact it is a Festiniog train approaching Waenfawr from the south. The WHR was little used by villagers, as the buses ran direct to Caernarvon, a destination sought by the WHR promoters but opposed by the LNWR. (R.Shephard coll./WHR)

SOUTH OF WAENFAWR

16.   One mile south, a station was provided at Bettws Garmon, but the once important iron ore traffic here had ceased in 1920 and the siding was removed in 1922. Nearby a slate quarry was re-opened briefly in 1933. Here *Moel Tryfan* runs north with a NWNG bogie brake composite and two open coaches passing over the Afon Gwyrfai. Although photographed in about 1892, the stock and scenery were little changed in the 1920s. Further north, Salem Halt was opened on 21st July 1922 and a ballast siding constructed. Plas-y-Nant was also provided with a halt. (A.Rimmer coll./WHR)

QUELLYN LAKE

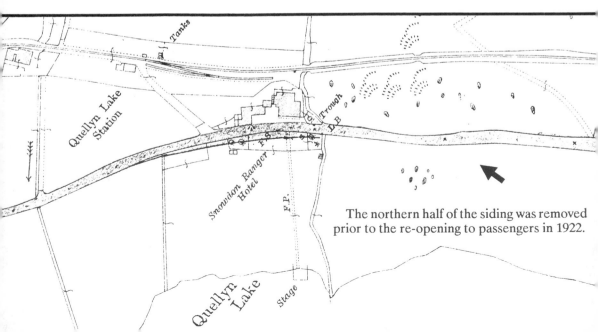

The northern half of the siding was removed prior to the re-opening to passengers in 1922.

17.   After running parallel to the mile-long lake, the railway reached Quellyn Lake station, a name used initially and also during the WHR era. During the latter days of the NWNGR it was "Snowdon Ranger". This westward view was recorded just before the opening of the WHR, the disarmed signal being of NWNGR origin and superfluous with a Light Railway Order. The station building was just beyond the right margin of the picture. (Gwynedd Archives Service/WHR)

18.   The station building (centre) was well preserved when photographed in March 1992. It had not suffered the addition of new buildings with which many historic stations have been plagued. Here the formation is just over 500ft above sea level. (V.Mitchell)

SOUTH SNOWDON

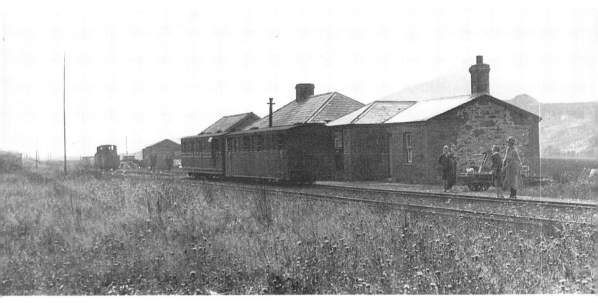

19.   Until 1922 this was the southern terminus of the NWNGR and was named Rhyd-Ddu (Black Ford) after the village nearby. For twelve months from October 1922 the station was misleadingly named just "Snowdon". This 1925 view shows an England engine detached from its train, probably running round. (C.Mowat)

In the summer of 1927, a train from Portmadoc terminated here at 11.59am, returning at 12.4. In 1928 there were two such workings. The line was in use southwards during WWI for timber traffic, using part of the incomplete PB&SSR.

16th February 1928. Bad timings due to poor steaming ... tubes covered with some stuff like glue ... small coal sticks to it ... tubes must be cleaned every journey ... this takes much time ...

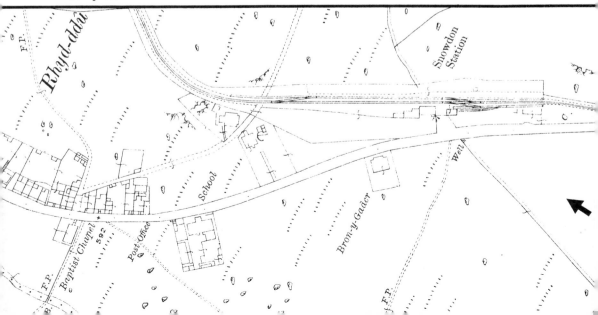

20. While the guttering and downpipe were in disarray on the west elevation, the leaning sign announced to early motorists the existence of a "parking ground" at the enormous charge of one shilling, equivalent to over £3 today. The entire site is now a public car park and no trace of the building remains.
(RAS Marketing/WHR)

21. Another 1939 view shows that 10ins high cast iron letters were still in place but that much of the rather more useful guttering had gone by then. During the final years of operation it was the guard's duty to lock and unlock the waiting room. No signal box was ever provided, the few signals in use prior to 1916 being controlled from the main building.
(WHR coll.)

22. After passing over the summit, just south of Pitt's Head Halt, the line took a sinuous course, descending mostly at 1 in 40 and passing Hafod Ruffydd Halt two miles before reaching Beddgelert. The locomotive is 2-6-2T *Russell*, with complete dome, cab and chimney before being cut down to FR loading gauge early in 1925. (P.Johnson coll.)

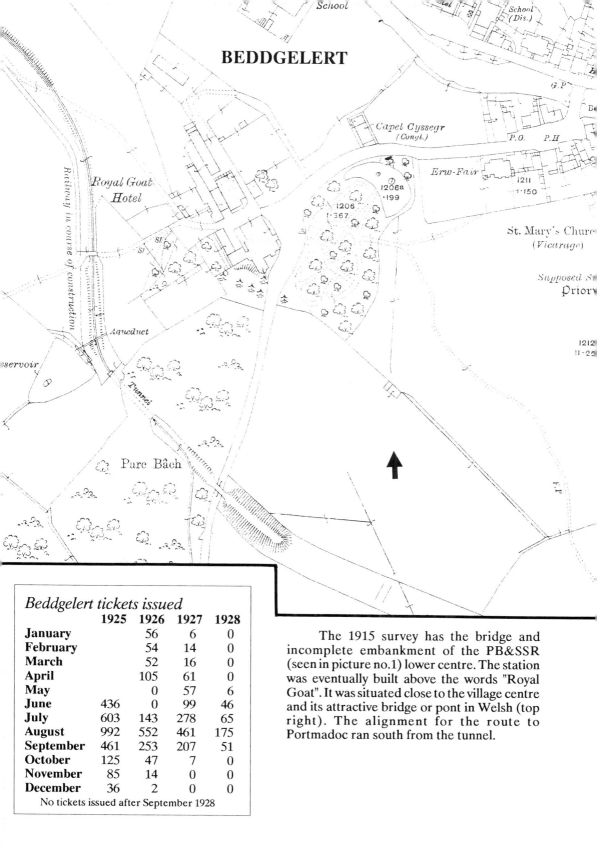

BEDDGELERT

School

School (Dis.)

G.P

Capel Cyssegr (Congl.)

P.O.   P.H

Erw-Fair

1211

·150

Royal Goat Hotel

1206a ·199

1206 1·367

St. Mary's Churc (Vicarage)

Railway in course of construction

Supposed S Priory

Aqueduct

1212 11·25

servoir

Tunnel

Parc Bâch

The 1915 survey has the bridge and incomplete embankment of the PB&SSR (seen in picture no.1) lower centre. The station was eventually built above the words "Royal Goat". It was situated close to the village centre and its attractive bridge or pont in Welsh (top right). The alignment for the route to Portmadoc ran south from the tunnel.

23. The station was set amidst beautiful scenery and was equipped with a bookshop (lower right), no doubt of value to some passengers during the lengthy waits at this location. It was blown over in a gale in October 1927 and subsequently sold for £5. The train that has just arrived in this 1925 view is composed of FR bogie coaches with one of that company's original batch of four-wheelers. The locomotive has left the train to take water before running round. (F.Frith/WHR)

24. On the left is *Russell*, displaying its cab as mutilated during Col. Stephens' term of office. The engine was devoid of a rear cab sheet in the summer of 1925. On the right stands the bargain ex-WD locomotive, no.590, which was prone to poor performance and was unpopular with the crews. Also evident is one of the partially glazed tourist coaches. (Lens of Sutton/WHR)

WHR 17   RUSSELL AND 590 AT BEDDGELERT c1930   Photo LENS OF SUTTON

25. In 1922 this was the entire locomotive stock of the WHR. Seen on the left in 1935 is 0-6-4T *Moel Tryfan* and alongside is 2-6-2T *Russell*, both carrying drums of sand for application by the fireman who had to ride on the buffer beam in slippery conditions. (J.E.Simpson/WHR)

26. *Little Giant* has just arrived from Portmadoc and adds to the smoke from the chimneys of the Royal Goat Hotel, left. In the later years the practice was to operate the WHR as two railways - south of Beddgelert an FR crew and stock was used, while the line northwards was worked by a Dinas Junction-based crew with WHR stock. (Colonel Stephens Railway Archive)

27. A 1932 photograph illustrates the "frontier station" effect, with *Russell* and WHR coaches on the right and *Welsh Pony*, with FR stock on the left. The coal is in bogie wagons manufactured by Hudsons and acquired ex-WD after WWI. By the engine is Miriam Jones in Welsh national costume, emulating the then famous station mistress at Tanybwlch. (WHR coll.)

28. Taken in 1934, this picture includes a rare glimpse of one of the six short-lived Hudson-built tourist vehicles, used on both lines. A replica is now running again on the FR. The driver appears to be praying by the injector. This would have been necessary on many occasions as there are reports of failure of this vital component in mid-section and passengers having to walk thereafter. The cab boards were added in Wales. The shelf below them carried a suction hose for lifting water from a ditch or river - see picture 34. (F.C.LeManquais/Steamchest)

29. This poor snap from 1936 is included as it encapsulates so much action. The fireman of *Russell* is about to apply the handbrake as he runs in from the north while no.590 is still on the same line presumably in the process of running round a train that it has just brought up from Portmadoc. The coalman is filling sacks on his lorry. (H.B.Tours/WHR)

30. Next to *Little Giant* is no.2 of 1873 (now no.10) and no.17 of 1876, both coaches still being owned by the FR to this day. Partially obscuring the goods shed is a former FR quarrymen's coach, converted for use as a brake van and fitted with both vacuum and air pressure hoses as the FR used the former system and the WHR the latter.
(Colonel Stephens Railway Archive)

31. Long waits here were timetabled - even longer waits were common in the final years due to poor fuel, low maintenance and numerous other reasons. In November 1934 a local person was offered 2/6 a week to man the station, but he replied that he was worth five shillings, especially as engine cleaners earned £1 and drivers over £3 at that time. (WHR coll.)

32. The loop was on a gradient of 1 in 43, increasing to 1 in 40 down in this cutting at the south end of the station. The first bridge carries a footpath and farm track, the second being an aqueduct. Out of view is a short tunnel, 43yds in length. (F.C.LeManquais/Steamchest)

33. No.590 is northbound, half a mile south of Beddgelert, and is about to pass over the Afon Glaslyn on Bryn-y-Felin bridge. Beyond it is an embankment and a bridge which caries the A487 over the railway. All structures were still visible in 1992. (S.W.Baker/WHR)

34. The Pass of Aberglaslyn narrows for nearly a mile, forcing the railway engineers to tunnel in part of the most scenic section and deprive passengers of some splendid views of the gorge. No.590 heads a train from Portmadoc in 1925 and is emerging from the 17yd long tunnel. The one in the distance is 300yds in length; a third (behind the camera) is 37yds long. (F.Frith/A.Gray coll.)

35.   At the south end of the Pass of
Aberglaslyn, the line enters Nantmor Cutting,
still falling at 1 in 40. Superb scenery surrounds
Russell but passengers have to be content with
a close examination of geological structures in
this vicinity.
(Colonel Stephens Railway Archive)

NANTMOR

36.   Moel Hebog is in the background as *Princess* displays spare steam upon arrival from Portmadoc with a train formation identical to that seen in picture no. 23. The fresh, neat appearance suggests a date of about 1923-24. (WHR coll.)

37.   *Russell* approaches the solitary siding, which has upturned rails as stops. The coal yard here closed in March 1925, having been used by Mr. Roberts. A bicycle leans against the corrugated iron clad building, which was typical of those used on the other lines controlled by Colonel Stephens. South of Nantmor there were halts at Hafod-y-Llyn, Hafod Garegog and Ynysferlas but the last two were not in use simultaneously. (WHR coll.)

CROESOR JUNCTION

38. A northward view in 1925 shows the main line to Beddgelert curving to the left and wagons standing on the horse-worked Croesor Tramway, which ran for about three miles to slate quarries in the Croesor Valley. It was in use from 1863/64 until 1930. The former four-wheel coach was used as a waiting room. Records show several cancellations of the Fridays-only market train between Portmadoc and Croesor Junction in the winter of 1928, due to "tractor failure". It ran at 11.45am from Croesor Junction and 4.0pm from Portmadoc, but its duration of operation is not recorded. (C.Mowat)

The line south to Portmadoc was completely relaid to higher standards for locomotive use but the junction layout was not approved. It was relaid in 1924 so that traffic from Croesor could pass from Croesor Junction to Portmadoc using the staff for that section, whereas the first layout necessitated use of the Beddgelert-Croesor Junction staff. A telephone and locked cabinet for train staff tickets were housed in the old coach body.

To Stephens from Evans 7th June 1927.

I beg to report that the workings of the WHR yesterday were very bad. The 2.14pm from Portmadoc did not arrive at Dinas until 5.24pm, practically an hour late. It lost the connection with the LMS at 4.43pm and there were passengers for Colwyn Bay. The 4.45pm from Dinas left 1hr 7mins late. I had made arrangements for 5.5pm from Portmadoc for to go on to Waenfawr to pass the 4.45 there. Owing to the telephone not working properly, I was very anxious about the train. No sign of the train could be seen at South Snowdon; eventually it arrived at 7.58pm after stopping with engine trouble Having failed to get any water at Quellyn Lake, the driver had no alternative but to take the fire from the engine.

I had to get in touch with Mr Willliams at Boston Lodge as regards working a special as far as Beddgelert to fetch the passengers that had been waiting there from 6 o'clock. He had no driver on duty, only a fireman and so he himself went with a small engine at 8.30. The train got back to Portmadoc at 10.15pm. There were passengers for Penrhyn so I sent the train on to Minffordd. Luckily there were none for Festiniog. I do not know whether the best was done by the enginemen on the Baldwin which caused so much delay. It is most important for the telephone to be in working order ......

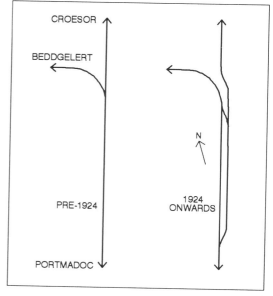

YNYSFOR

39. A halt with siding was established 600yds south of Croesor Junction, the simple facilities being recorded in about 1925 in this damaged view towards Croesor Junction. Some milk churn traffic was recorded at this halt which is situated on the flat pastures of the reclaimed estuary. (C.Mowat)

40. A southward view in about 1939 shows the up-turned rail at the end of the siding (lower right) and Y Garth, the granite outcrop north of Minffordd on the left. (R.Shephard)

PONT CROESOR

41. A northward view after closure shows the water tank on the Merioneth bank of the Glaslyn. The halt, together with a trailing siding on the west side of the line, is behind the camera. The road is the B4410 from Prenteg to Llanfrothen. Half a mile to the south was Pont Rhyddin Halt, the site of a passing loop in horse-worked time. After 1924 this became a south facing siding, used for loading sand. The railway was dismantled during WWII but the road bridge is still in use. (R.Shephard)

PORTMADOC
BEDDGELERT SIDING

42. An interesting, although poor, southward view from 1932 has Portmadoc in the background and the transhipment shed partially obscured by a van. Standard gauge wagons are on the right. (W.D.Miller/WHR)

Portmadoc New tickets issued	1925	1926	1927	1928	1929	1930	1931	1932	1933	1934	1935	1936
January		392	0	121						0	0	0
February		268	0	94						0	0	0
March		323	169	104						0	0	0
April		577	202	62						0	0	0
May		42	259	96	Despite repeated requests from					0	0	0
June	1467	0	560	114	Tonbridge, Portmadoc ignored					0	0	0
July	1660	574	873	261	these and made no returns for					618	631	1205
August	3336	2171	1696	1071	the years 1929 to 1933					2 911	2753	2628
September	1770	989	1017	145						1 056	438	560
October	627	0	43	0						0	0	0
November	488	0	53	0						0	0	0
December	339	0	140	0						0	0	0

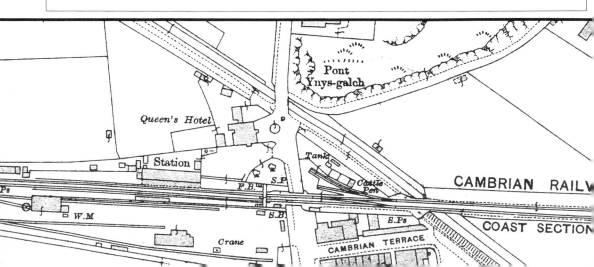

43. Looking north, in about 1925, we see some of the stock of the Rhosydd Slate Quarry, a large quarry at the head of the Croesor Valley, which closed for the third time in September 1930. The main line from Croesor Junction is on the right. (C.Mowat)

Top right is the line from Croesor Junction and the exchange sidings with the standard gauge Cambrian Railway, which became part of the GWR in 1922. The WHR's Portmadoc New station was built near the lower right border of this map in 1923. The route of the standard gauge siding from below the word *CAMBRIAN* to the top right corner is now the site of the present WHR operation. The field in the south-east angle between the GWR and WHR was acquired by the FR for the construction of a new works to replace Boston Lodge.

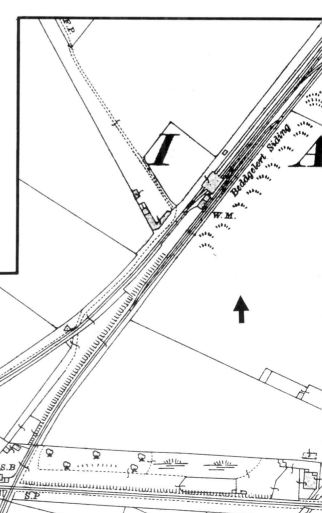

PORTMADOC

NEW 1929

44. Portmadoc New was established south of the GWR crossing, but after five years of frustration with that company regarding excessive charges for, and delays at, the crossing, the WHR terminated most trains north of the main line. We look south from that point, the GWR signal box being beyond the end of the train. The gable end of the 1923 station is to the left of the box, the black square representing the water tank. The tall building on the left is the flour mill, which was rail served. (W.G.Rear coll./WHR)

Labour	11 - 6
Use of telegraph	17 - 4 - 11
Clothing	1 - 4 - 2
Stores	9
Oil for lights	18 - 3
Maintenance of clock	1 - 9
Totals	**£ 20 - 2 - 2**

This bill from Paddington was for the six months to 30th June 1930. At this time there were fewer than ten wagons per week crossing, mostly traffic between the flour mill and Beddgelert siding. Investigation showed that the clock was missing.

45. The GWR signal box is on the right again. The station comprised a second hand waiting shed and an unsatisfactory loop on which locomotives were liable to derail. Because of this, the crews normally hauled the coaches into it by means of a thick rope (probably that seen in picture no.8), thus keeping the engine (in this case *Russell*) on the main line. The loop is marked on the map near the words "Beddgelert Siding". (S.W.Baker)

PORTMADOC
GWR CROSSING

46. *Russell* proceeds north on 8th July 1936 and passes the 1923 signal box, which contained six levers, two for narrow gauge trap points and four for main line signals. Regular passenger trains over the crossing were reinstated in 1935-36. Until 1923 it was regarded as a simple occupation crossing and a cottage was provided for a crossing keeper, often a woman. With the advent of narrow gauge passenger trains and control of the main line from Paddington, the GWR imposed exorbitant charges of over £150 per annum, without any legal justification. (S.W.Baker)

47. The point rod to the northern trap point is evident in this 1934 photograph, as is a line of wagons stored in the Beddgelert siding, by then not used for transfer purposes. A stile can be seen to the right of the gate. The WHR reduced costs by hiring the GWR porter/signalman for two or three 15 minute periods each day, instead of paying for full time staff, thus allowing wagons and/or FR stock to cross. (C.J.Keylock coll.)

PORTMADOC
NEW 1923

48. Looking north we see the GWR signal box beyond the gates which protected the crossing. The slate edged platforms are also evident, as is the station building (left), which was purchased for £75 ex-Army. (C.Mowat)

49. A more distant view of the same site includes the full length of the loop and the refreshment room, the long boarded building on the left. Adjacent to it is the freshly surfaced approach road. (A.Gray coll./WHR)

50. The driver leans against *Palmerston*, while the fireman directs local passengers to the connecting train, using a cigarette for the purpose, "Over two stiles, unless the gate has been left unlocked!" he was probably remarking. The date is 29th July 1924. (R.B.Moulndale)

Traffic report - 7th June 1929.
2-50pm to Blaenau Ffestiniog delayed until 3.4pm awaiting the shunting over the GWR of a van loaded with furniture from Hafod Ruffydd to Dduallt.

```
┌─────────────────────────────────────────┐
│      WELSH HIGHLAND RAILWAY.         ┌──┐│
│  NOTICE.- This Ticket is issued subject to│
│  the conditions & regulations in the Com-│
│  panys Time Tables, Books Bills & Notices.│
│            DINAS             ┌──┐    │
│             TO               │122│   │
│     BLAENAU FESTINIOG                 │
│    Third Class Actual Fare 5/5        │
└─────────────────────────────────────────┘
```

WELSH HIGHLAND RAILWAY.
NOTICE.- This Ticket is issued subject to the conditions & regulations in the Companys Time Tables, Books Bills & Notices.
DINAS
TO
BLAENAU FESTINIOG
Third Class Actual Fare **5/5**
122

51. The guard leans out as *Prince* overflows from its injector and the rear four-wheeler passes over the GWR. During 1929-30 this station saw little traffic, as passengers were expected to walk through the town if making a journey. The crossing was removed in 1938. (Gwynedd Archives Service)

PORTMADOC
JUNCTION RAILWAY

H. P. to which
O. T. flow

W. M

Chy.

Corn Mill

L.B

C°

North Wales
Slate Works

W. M.

Sawmill
Terrace

Chapel

Infant
School

Sunday
School

Drill
Hall

Smithy

STREET

MADOC

STREET

SNOWDON

STREET

CROESOR TRAMWAY

F.P.

SMITH STREET

P.H

P.H.

P.H.

Club

IE PARK

Meth
apel

Smithy

Ynys-tywyn

PORTMADOC

Lock Gates

Ynys Tywyn

The work of upgrading the Croesor
Tramway through the town was undertaken
under a FR Light Railway Order of 30th
January 1923. The top of this map joins with
the bottom of the previous one and shows a
roof over double track by the mill. The roof was
removed as it was unauthorised and reduced
clearances. The loop was to have been
converted to a siding but seems to have been
retained as a loop. The siding on the left had
once been part of the Gorseddau Railway. The
siding on the lower part of the route enters the
Glaslyn Foundry. This area is now the site of
the main car park and supermarket. At the
lower border, the line runs towards the
wharves. A new line was added in 1923 to give
a direct link with the FR.

52. The northern points of the flour mill loop were on the bridge over Y Cyt, formerly the Tremadoc Canal. This post-closure view shows the water tank support in front of the crossing keeper's cottage, the signal box having been demolished in 1938. (LGRP)

53. A horse stands at the head of a train of flat wagons, probably loaded with flour for transhipment at Beddgelert siding. The unauthorised roof and the remains of the Gorseddau Railway are also evident, its second track later becoming disused and buried. This photograph was taken prior to 1923, by which time the steam powered mill was producing 6000 tons of flour per annum, mostly despatched by rail. (C.J.Keylock coll.)

54. The southern part of the flour mill loop and the revised loading shelter are on the right. The remains of the Gorseddau Railway (left) served to carry slate blocks and slabs to the works nearby. (LGRP)

55. Slate wagons (left) lie abandoned at the North Wales Slate Company's premises and the Gorseddau Railway goes no further. It joined Y Cyt at the far end of the works (on the right) and crossed the main line on the level near the Cambrian Railways station. (R.K.Cope/R.S.Carpenter)

56.   A view up Madoc Street shows the 1923
route entering the main road. The Croesor
Tramway (shown on the map) continued to the
left border of this picture, that direct
connection to the wharves being lifted in April
1928. The wall on the right had to be set back
in 1923 - it was later removed to give access to
a petrol filling station. (LGRP)

57.   *Russell* approaches the High Street on 8th
July 1936 with the 10.45am from Dinas. On the
left is a sign of the times and the main reason
for the decline in rail traffic. Crosville
commenced running buses to Blaenau
Ffestiniog for quarrymen in September 1927.
(S.W.Baker)

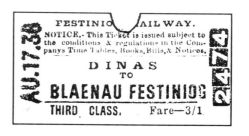

FESTINIOG RAILWAY.

NOTICE.- This Ticket is issued subject to
the conditions & regulations in the Companys Time Tables, Books, Bills,& Notices.

DINAS
TO
BLAENAU FESTINIOG
THIRD CLASS.   Fare—3/1

AU.17.36

P2474

58. A train emerges from Madoc Street, surrounded by steam leaking from *Merddin Emrys*. Double engines seldom ran north of the GWR, although two were coupled together on a test run from Beddgelert on 24th May 1923. They also ran some scheduled trains in 1924. On the left are sidings to the wharves and in the background is the Town Hall clock tower. (P.Johnson coll.)

59. No.590 faces the Maenofferen Quarry offices on 8th August 1935, as it crosses the High Street to head north. This engine had a high centre of gravity and gave crews a rough ride, adding to its unpopularity. Moreover, the often-resented Stephens had forced it upon them. Most of the Junction Railway was lifted in 1949 but the part on the Britannia Bridge remained until 1957. (H.F.Wheeller)

60. Looking in the other direction from about the same point, but many years later, we see the parapet walls of Britannia Bridge. The bridge had to be widened and strengthened in 1923, to accommodate passenger trains. The Junction Railway is in the foreground and wharf lines are on the right. In 1992, only the slate gate post on the right remained as evidence of a former railway presence here. It was deeply grooved by passing slate wagons owing to zero clearance. (LGRP)

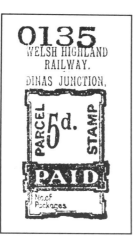

Tons of slate shipped	
1923	3112
1924	3446
1925	3510
1926	2265
1927	1894
1928	2653
1929	1814
1930	2117
1931	1483
1932	1632
1933	3638
1934	3478
1935	1489
1936	1563
1937	1873
1938	1491
1939	1700
1940	-
1941	-
1942	593
1943	-
1944	-
1945	-
1946	-

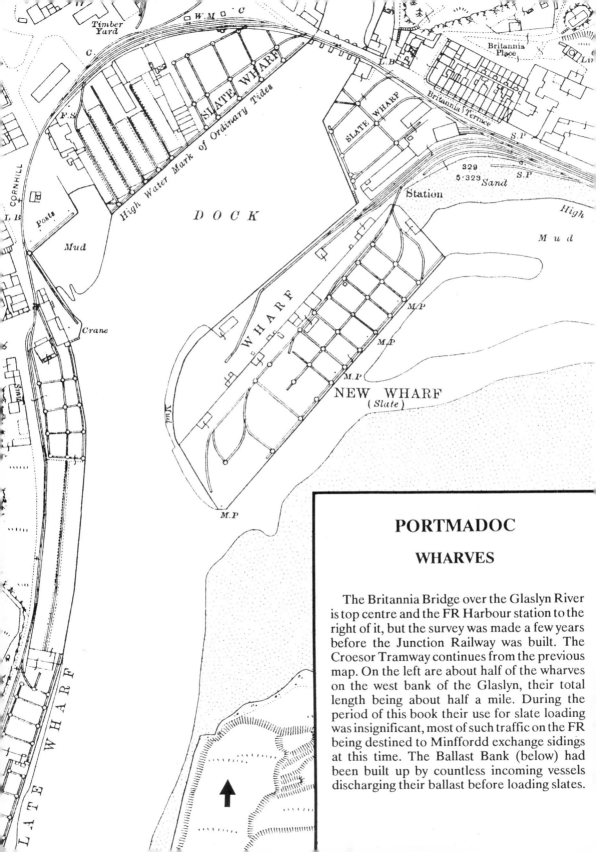

PORTMADOC

WHARVES

The Britannia Bridge over the Glaslyn River is top centre and the FR Harbour station to the right of it, but the survey was made a few years before the Junction Railway was built. The Croesor Tramway continues from the previous map. On the left are about half of the wharves on the west bank of the Glaslyn, their total length being about half a mile. During the period of this book their use for slate loading was insignificant, most of such traffic on the FR being destined to Minffordd exchange sidings at this time. The Ballast Bank (below) had been built up by countless incoming vessels discharging their ballast before loading slates.

61. The schooners of earlier years gave way to steamships. Here the *S.S.Holyhead* loads slates at Garth Quay. In more prosperous days, slate had been conveyed to Germany, North America and further afield, but alternative manufactured roofing materials and the effects of WWI on shipping had brought about a decline in traffic. (FR coll.)

62. The line to most of the wharves passed along the highway across Cornhill (top left on the map), an apt name in view of the tonnage of grain landed here to feed the residents of this mountainous district, unable to grow their own. Most was shipped from Liverpool, with some coming from Belfast, presumably transferred there from ocean going vessels. The FR zero mile post was in the background. (C.Mowat)

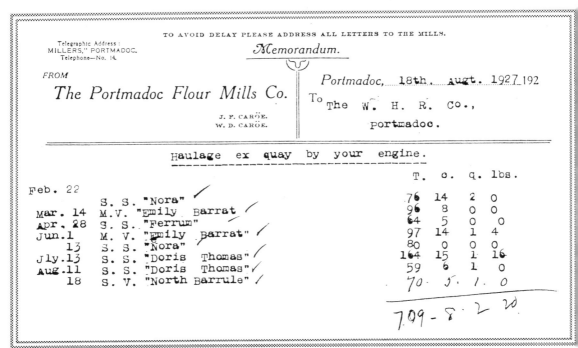

Telegraphic Address :
MILLERS," PORTMADOC.
Telephone—No. 14.

Memorandum.

FROM

The Portmadoc Flour Mills Co.

J. F. CARÖE.
W. D. CARÖE.

Portmadoc, 18th. Augt. 1927 192

To The W. H. R. Co.,

portmadoc.

Haulage ex quay by your engine.

		T.	c.	q.	lbs.
Feb. 22	S. S. "Nora"	76	14	2	0
Mar. 14	M.V. "Emily Barrat	96	8	0	0
Apr. 28	S. S. "Ferrum"	64	5	0	0
Jun. 1	M. V. "Emily Barrat"	97	14	1	4
13	S. S. "Nora"	80	0	0	0
Jly. 13	S. S. "Doris Thomas"	164	15	1	16
Aug. 11	S. S. "Doris Thomas"	59	6	1	0
18	S. V. "North Barrule"	70	5	1	0

709 - 8 . 2 . 20

An average of 500 tons of grain per month was imported in 1923, this dwindling to 100 by 1927. It was usually hauled by a FR petrol tractor to the mill. Flour was conveyed from there to Penrhyn by rail in substantial quantities. About one ton went each week to Beddgelert.

63. *Taliesin* is propelling wagons towards Cornhill in the 1930s, although it was normal for smaller engines to shunt the wharves. Double engines were not allowed to cross the Britannia Bridge until it was widened and strengthened in 1923. The points on the left are shown on the map, south-west of the timber yard. The location is close to the present coach park. (FR coll.)

PORTMADOC
OLD

64.   When photographed in July 1936 the wharves were showing no signs of commercial activity. On the right is the FR Harbour Station, generally known as "Portmadoc Old" during the period of operation of the WHR, that is 1923-36. (S.W.Baker)

65.   A train from Portmadoc New stands parallel to Britannia Terrace (marked top right on the map). The locomotive is *Merddin Emrys*. A coaling stage was established here for the benefit of crews working through trains. It did not endear the railway to the nearby residents who suffered dust and clouds of sulphurous yellow smoke from cheap imported Belgian coal. (P.Johnson coll.)

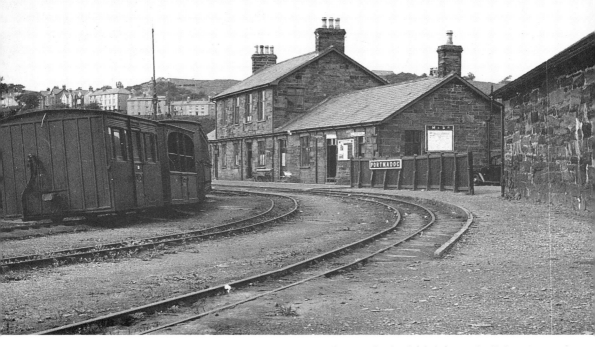

66. The old established platform was used by passengers visiting the booking office and/or the toilets, and stock was stored in the sidings. The goods shed (right) was built in 1878-79, as was the station building. The curve is on a 2-chain radius. (G.F.Parker)

Ordinary tickets

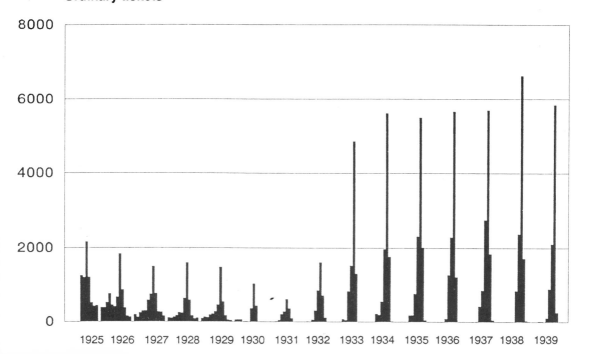

PORTMADOC
HARBOUR

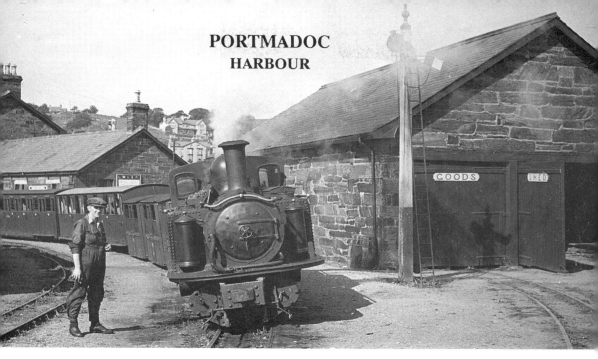

67.   As the 1920s progressed, so the station became more frequently used by FR trains, fewer running through to Portmadoc New or beyond. Note that *Taliesin* has the original type of buffer and wagon hook, rather than the now familiar Norwegian-style chopper coupling. This is a post 1932 view. (G.F.Parker)

Portmadoc		
1946	**Goods outward** Tons	**Minerals inwards** Tons
January	6	8
February	1	4
March	4	19
April	2	5
May	1	54
June	2	53
July	6	23
	No other traffic recorded	

Workmans tickets

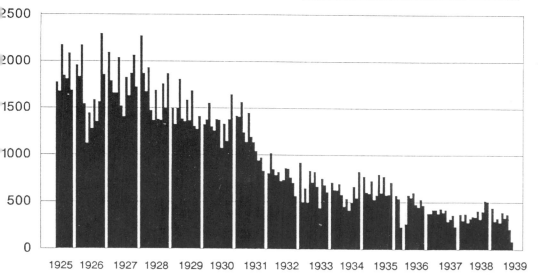

68. An oil lamp shows lack of modernisation of the station, while some movement with the times is revealed by the sign *YOU MAY TELEPHONE FROM HERE* on the booking office wall. The intricate coach panelling is a legacy of more prosperous days. (FR coll.)

69. A 1934 photograph of the end of the line includes *Merddin Emrys* and the unusual three-way stub point. This type was first installed here in 1879. This set was moved to Boston Lodge in 1964 and since 1987 has been in use near the carriage shed at Minffordd. (F.C.LeManquais/Steamchest)

70. *Taliesin* heads a FR train while *Russell* waits to draw its WHR train onto the Cob, run round it, and proceed to Beddgelert in 1936, the final year of that line's operation. In June 1937, *Russell's* final task was to haul the partially dismantled Baldwin, no.590, from Boston Lodge to Dinas Junction, where they are seen together in picture no.8. (S.W.Baker)

71. By the time this photograph was taken, in May 1937, the station name had reverted to "Harbour". In the distance are the sheds once used for slate storage on the wharves. One of the four-wheelers is accompanied by two of the second batch of bogie coaches, plus a converted bogie brake van. On the left is the now long forgotten siding to South Snowdon New Wharf. (H.A.K.Smith/FR coll.)

PORTMADOC
THE COB

72. Just as a rousing overture prepares one for a great musical performance, so the journey across The Cob can create a sense of anticipation of the scenic joys to come. *Taliesin* heads east on 8th July 1936, carrying some of the last passengers to enjoy (or endure) the anti-clockwise railtour of North Wales. A low concrete wall was added in 1939 to the seaward side of the Cob. (S.W.Baker)

73. Sleeper replacement work stops as a double engine approaches with two bogies and two four-wheelers in 1936. It is passing the long carriage siding which was lifted in 1939 during embankment repairs. In the distance is the quarry from where rock was obtained for the construction of The Cob, this being completed in July 1811. (S.W.Baker)

74. A 1935 view towards Portmadoc shows that The Cob carried not only a road and a railway, but two telephone systems. The FR's (seen better in the previous picture) had seven wires and the GPO route had so many as to give crossed lines in strong winds. They were soon to be put underground. Until 1929 the signal gantry had controlled the approach to Duffws. (A.Gray coll.)

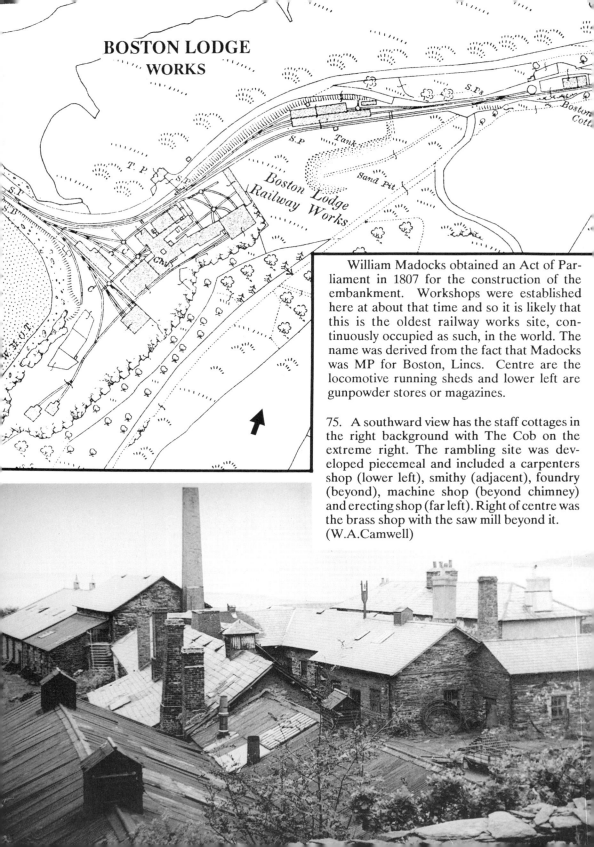

BOSTON LODGE
WORKS

Boston Lodge Railway Works

William Madocks obtained an Act of Parliament in 1807 for the construction of the embankment. Workshops were established here at about that time and so it is likely that this is the oldest railway works site, continuously occupied as such, in the world. The name was derived from the fact that Madocks was MP for Boston, Lincs. Centre are the locomotive running sheds and lower left are gunpowder stores or magazines.

75. A southward view has the staff cottages in the right background with The Cob on the extreme right. The rambling site was developed piecemeal and included a carpenters shop (lower left), smithy (adjacent), foundry (beyond), machine shop (beyond chimney) and erecting shop (far left). Right of centre was the brass shop with the saw mill beyond it. (W.A.Camwell)

76. A 1936 view from The Cob includes the staff cottages (left, with stables in front), the pattern loft (right of chimney) and the gable end of the long shed or paint shop, behind the engine. Behind that building is the erecting shop. Until WWI a ramped roadway ran through the arch (centre) up into the bottom yard. (S.W.Baker)

78. Seen in the works in 1934 is a petrol tractor (using the parlance of the era) built by Pittsburgh Model Engine Co. under licence from the Baldwin Locomotive Co. for use in France in WWI. Purchased by the FR in 1925, it was abortively fitted with vacuum equipment in 1928 to work winter trains on the WHR. The name *Moelwyn* was applied in 1956. This is a punning allusion to "Baldwin" - Moel = bald. (A.Gray coll.)

77. In the 1930s a number of historic relics littered Glan-y-mor yard, south of the works. No.6, an original four-wheeler is in the company of the remains of 0-4-4T single Fairlie *Taliesin* of 1876, always a popular engine and withdrawn from traffic in 1930. (R.G.Jarvis)

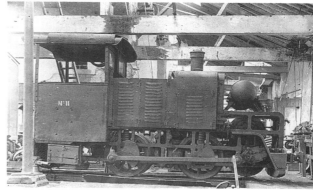

BOSTON LODGE
LOCOMOTIVE SHEDS

79. Owing to congestion in the works, a separate running shed was built in 1863 and extended at the far end in 1892 - 93. The shed on the left had been added by 1887. Seen from left to right in June 1932 are the main road, the Afon Glaslyn, Y Garth (granite quarry), the running sheds and the main line climbing towards Minffordd. This was the FR's centenary year, the event being marked by a feature programme on the "wireless". (H.C.Casserley)

80. A closer look on 31st August 1926 shows *Palmerston* being prepared and *Prince* approaching. England engines were commonly used for shunting at each end of the FR, the top shunter serving the slate and granite quarries while the bottom shunter sorted wagons on the wharves at Portmadoc and Minffordd. (H.C.Casserley)

14th March 1928. Fireman late on duty ... 5-30 instead of 4.30am (had worked with bad coal until 6.45pm last night) ... quarrymen wild ...

81. The shed eventually became used for the storage of locomotives awaiting repair. Here there are two England engines, *Russell* and a double engine bogie. There was no electricity supply here or in the works at the time of closure. (W.A.Camwell)

21st February 1928. The quarrymen are getting very wild about the late running of their train ... 40 minutes taken to clear clinker and tubes ... strong complaints from drivers re coal ... quarrys need empty wagons held up ...

82. A sandpot lid covers one chimney as *Merddin Emrys* slumbers in the decaying shed in the 1930s. She was idle from 1915 to 1921, awaiting a new boiler. In 1934 the boiler was sent to the Avonside Engine Co. for major repairs and the locomotive (built in 1879 at Boston Lodge), along with *Princess* was still in use when the line closed in 1946. (R.G.Jarvis)

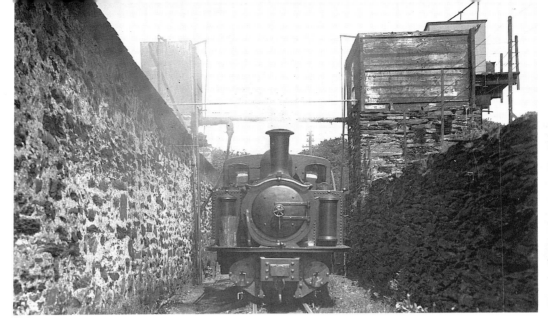

83. The long windowless wall is the one seen on the right of pictures 79 and 80. *Taliesin* was completed in 1886 by the FR and carried the name *Livingston Thompson* until 1932. The engine was laid up from 1924 until 1932 awaiting boiler repairs and was withdrawn again in 1939. (H.C.Casserley)

84. At the north east end of the sheds, the tracks converged and continued to a turntable. In addition to an Ashbury coach, we see the crane that Stephens purchased but that the railway never needed. It would not pass under the road bridge near the works. Its only recorded use was on sea wall repairs in 1939. The Lynton and Barnstaple Railway acquired *two* similar cranes - see our *Branch Line to Lynton*. The Cob and Portmadoc are in the distance. (H. F.Wheeller)

BOSTON LODGE
HALT

85. This photograph was taken from the same point as the previous one, but looking up the line in 1932. A wagon stands on the concealed 22ft turntable, the only other clue to its presence being the points in the main line, which were removed in 1944. The table was last used regularly in 1923. The path on the right leads to Portmeirion. The house was the residence of the locomotive superintendent for many years. (H.C.Casserley)

G.F.Williams recounts that he started in Boston Lodge Works at the age of 14 in 1919 and that his main tasks were cleaning the engine shed and making tea for over 40 men. He also had to sweep the machine shop, clean the offices and fetch the mail off the 10.55 train. He graduated to cooking food which the workers had brought with them, each having special requirements, such as fried bacon or fish, and following instructions written on eggs, some 20 of which had to be hard boiled, soft boiled or fried!

At 16 years of age, he became an engine cleaner, the hours being 10pm to 7am. He spent every night working on "Taliesin", the dome alone taking 1½ hours to polish.

Promotion to fireman came in 1923, the duty being on the bottom shunter, working to Minffordd and Portmadoc. Work on the top shunter followed but this involved sleeping in barracks at Blaenau Ffestiniog on alternate nights and starting work at 3am.

Firing passenger trains was eventually achieved. He did not complain at rising at 3.30am to be on duty at 4.30. He felt fortunate that he would be paid whether the engine was fit to run or not, as the quarrymen would loose a days pay if the train failed.

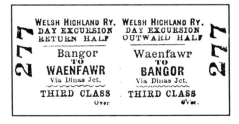

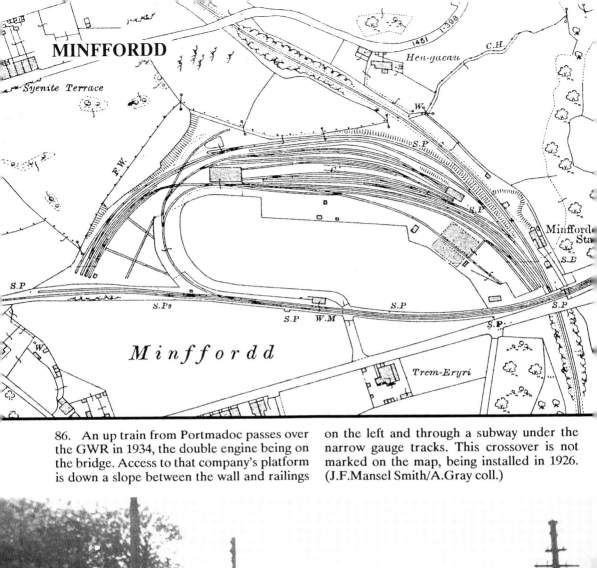

MINFFORDD

Syenite Terrace

Hen-gacau

Minffordd Sta.

Minffordd

Trem-Eryri

86.   An up train from Portmadoc passes over the GWR in 1934, the double engine being on the bridge. Access to that company's platform is down a slope between the wall and railings on the left and through a subway under the narrow gauge tracks. This crossover is not marked on the map, being installed in 1926. (J.F.Mansel Smith/A.Gray coll.)

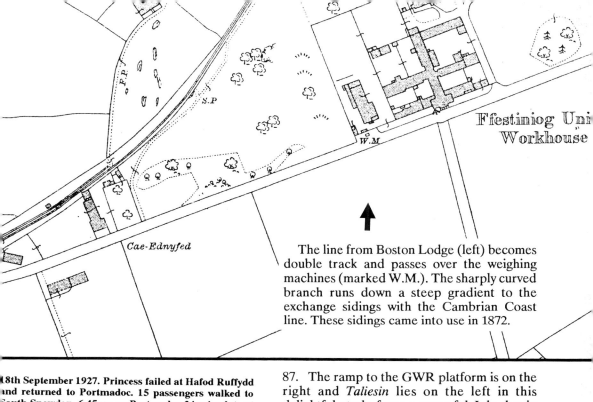

Ffestiniog Uni
Workhouse

S.P

W.M

Cae-Ednyfed

The line from Boston Lodge (left) becomes double track and passes over the weighing machines (marked W.M.). The sharply curved branch runs down a steep gradient to the exchange sidings with the Cambrian Coast line. These sidings came into use in 1872.

18th September 1927. Princess failed at Hafod Ruffydd and returned to Portmadoc. 15 passengers walked to South Snowdon. 6.45pm ex-Portmadoc 34 mins late at Blaenau. 4 passengers lost LMS connection. Took 10.5 SO to Dolwyddellan. Down passengers had to wait at Minffordd until 10.0pm for Pwllheli train. The fire of Princess was dropped in the middle of Cob due to injector failure.

87. The ramp to the GWR platform is on the right and *Taliesin* lies on the left in this delightful study from a peaceful July day in 1936. Left hand running on the loop was preferable as slate traffic could continue direct into the yard. The German style weighted point lever indicates the direction for which the points are set. (S.W.Baker)

88. This picture was taken a few minutes after the previous one. The GWR signal box obscures the pedestrian subway to the FR platforms. Behind the wagons on the right are FR sidings and the slate merchants' wharves. (S.W.Baker)

6th September 1927. Pwllheli evening connection lost at Minffordd. GW would not await 10 minutes. FR late running due to delays by the GW at Portmadoc crossing earlier in the day.

25th April 1928. Simplex not available for the 7.0am Portmadoc - Minffordd slate loaders train ... no other engines ... men went on 7.55 and lost quarter days pay ...

Ordinary tickets

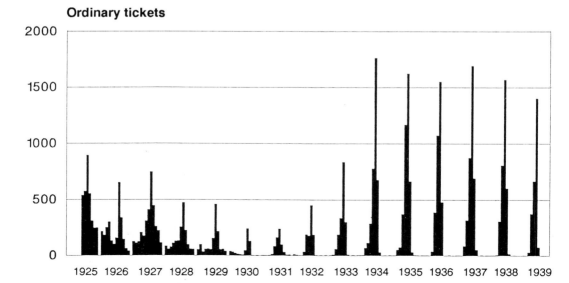

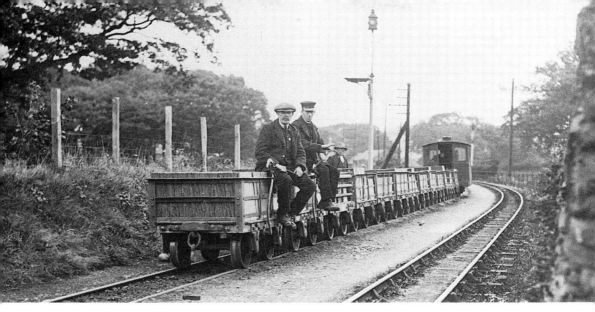

89.   Until 1939, loaded slate trains from Blaenau Ffestiniog were run down to Minffordd weigh house under gravity, the brakesmen here using ropes attached to the brake levers while another travels in the van. The train is only a few yards short of the weigh bridge. Note the rotatable signal lamp but the disc under it is not visible. Their use ceased in the 1920's. (P.Johnson coll.)

Minffordd		
1946	**Minerals outward**	**Minerals inwards**
	Tons	Tons
January	4	582
February	1	631
March	2	580
April	-	585
May	3	701
June	7	570
July	6	803

No other traffic recorded

Workmans tickets

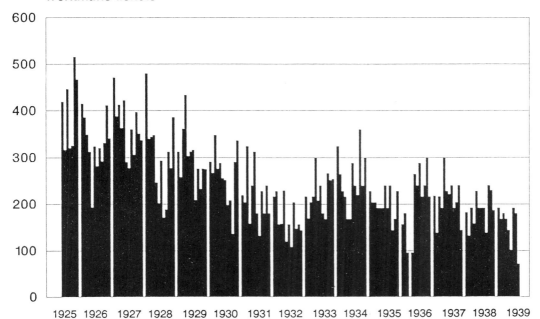

90. After weighing, the wagons descended this curve into the exchange sidings, where various slate merchants and quarries had stock yards. The granite quarry in the background was served by the GWR only. Wagons destined for Portmadoc Harbour were also weighed at Minffordd. (P.Johnson coll.)

91. The FR slate wagons mostly carried 2 tons, the main line ones being generally rated at 10. Large numbers of slate loaders travelled on the FR each day to and from Portmadoc. The hoop above the wagons was for supporting a tarpaulin sheet when required. (LGRP)

92. The yard came into use in 1872 and contained this large goods shed, used mainly for transhipment purposes. There was also a flour warehouse, but this was destroyed by fire on 6th August 1927. The locomotive is a Kerr Stuart 0-6-0 experimental diesel, fitted with a petrol engine to start it. It arrived on the WHR in July 1928 and was tried on the Bryngwyn branch. It was in use as a shunter on the FR from March until August of 1929 but was not economical and was returned to the maker after the trials. (R.C.Crick/FR coll.)

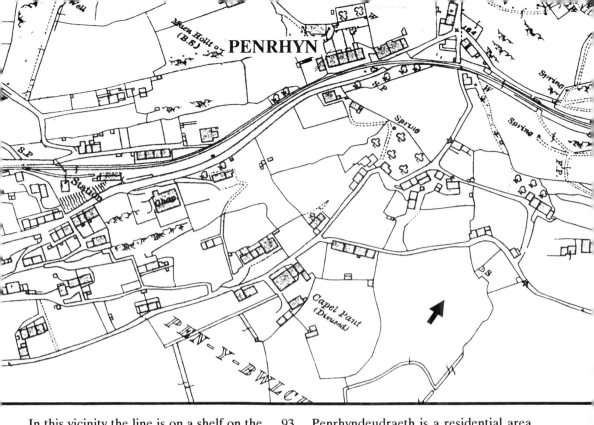

PENRHYN

In this vicinity the line is on a shelf on the hillside, a situation it maintains for most of the next six miles. A short siding is shown, this having been a loop for a brief period around 1912.

93. Penrhyndeudraeth is a residential area, once generating a large traffic in workmen travelling to the quarries. Although the doors of trains were locked, the quarrymen used their own keys, and are seen here ready to leap out before the train stops. (Mrs.G.Williams)

Ordinary tickets

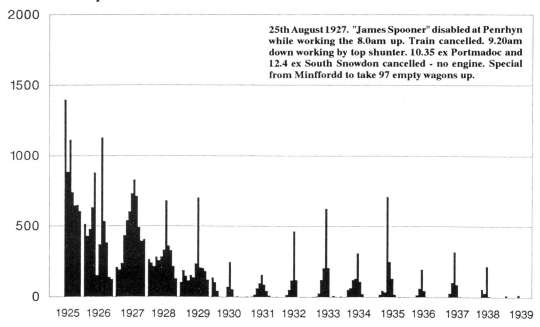

25th August 1927. "James Spooner" disabled at Penrhyn while working the 8.0am up. Train cancelled. 9.20am down working by top shunter. 10.35 ex Portmadoc and 12.4 ex South Snowdon cancelled - no engine. Special from Minffordd to take 97 empty wagons up.

94. The siding was used mainly for flour to the adjacent Co-op Bakery and is seen in 1938. The flour came from the mill at Portmadoc and also via the GWR at Blaenau Ffestiniog. Coal was seldom handled here, as it could be sent to the GWR station at the bottom of the town without transhipment. The centre vehicle is the six-wheeled Cleminson wagon no.8, a coal wagon which had been fitted with a roof in 1917 for flour traffic. The centre axle slid sideways on curves and was linked to the outer axles which pivoted to give a steering effect. Full details are given in *Branch Line to Southwold* - Middleton Press. (D.R.High coll.)

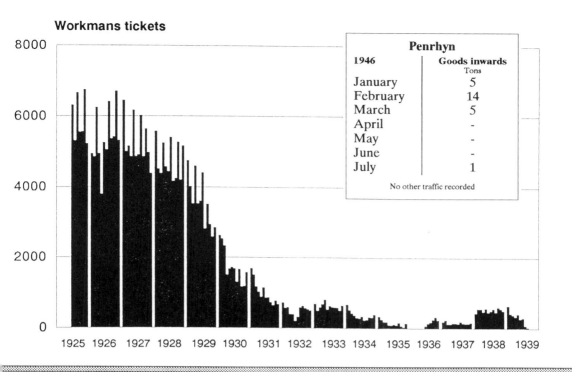

Workmans tickets

Penrhyn	
1946	**Goods inwards** Tons
January	5
February	14
March	5
April	-
May	-
June	-
July	1
	No other traffic recorded

EAST OF PENRHYN

95.   After climbing a further mile, passengers on the right of the four-wheelers were treated to the first of many splendid views of the Vale of Ffestiniog. Here they cross the 62ft high dry stone embankment, known as Cei Mawr. The small Birmingham coaches were always coupled next to the engine as they had softer drawbar springs than the bogie vehicles, thus reducing the shock on the engine when starting a long train. Another reason was that they had no brakes (only vacuum pipes) and so they had to be at the uphill end of the train in case of a breakaway.

(Colonel Stephens Railway Archives)

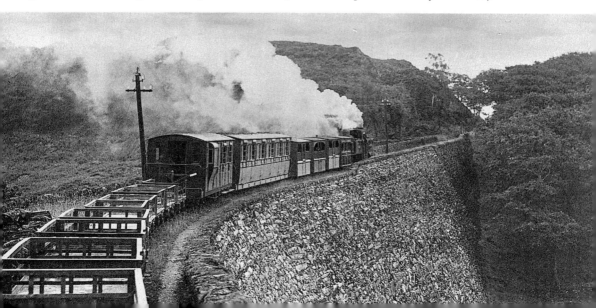

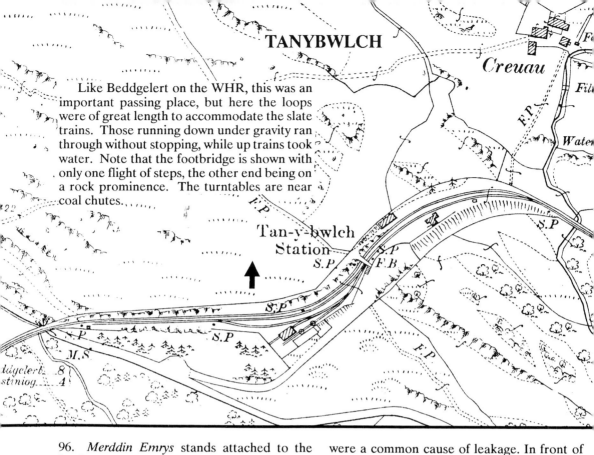

TANYBWLCH

Creuau

Tan-y-bwlch
Station

Like Beddgelert on the WHR, this was an important passing place, but here the loops were of great length to accommodate the slate trains. Those running down under gravity ran through without stopping, while up trains took water. Note that the footbridge is shown with only one flight of steps, the other end being on a rock prominence. The turntables are near coal chutes.

96. *Merddin Emrys* stands attached to the bogie van on its down train as *James Spooner* struggles up in poor condition on 4th August 1925. The flexible steam pipes to the bogies were a common cause of leakage. In front of the footbridge (demolished in 1933) is a slotted signal post which carried two arms until 1923. (H.G.W.Household)

97. The 1896 station house was added to in 1910 and by the 1930s it had become a popular source of tea, dispensed by Mrs. Bessie Jones, seen lower right. The early station building (left) continued to house the electric train staff equipment, a sophisticated system when compared with the wooden staffs used on most of the WHR. (FR coll.)

98. This view towards Blaenau Ffestiniog in about 1936 includes *Welsh Pony* and the water tank, which was filled with water from the hillside. This water was very acidic and is not suited to locomotive boilers or local stomachs. Non-stop gravity trains had the benefit of the larger radius curve. (FR coll.)

658	FESTINIOG RY.	FESTINIOG RY.	658
	Notice.- This Ticket is issued subject to the conditions on the Time Tables of the Company	RETURN HALF Notice.- This Ticket is issued subject to the conditions on the Time Tables of the Company	
	Dduallt TO MINFFORDD	Minffordd TO DDUALLT	
	Third Class 1/8	Third Class 1/8	

FESTINIOG RAILWAY.
NOTICE — This Ticket is issued subject to the conditions and regulations in the Companys Time Tables Books Bills and Notices.

MINFFORDD
TO
BLAENAU FFESTINIOG
SECOND CLASS Fare 1/10

4978

99.　Bessie Jones appears to be purveying postcards, probably of herself. She had acquired fame, as female station masters were uncommon and ones in Welsh costume were unheard of. In the background of this July 1936 picture is the 1883 goods shed and the crane, which was rated at 30cwt capacity. (S.W.Baker)

Ordinary tickets

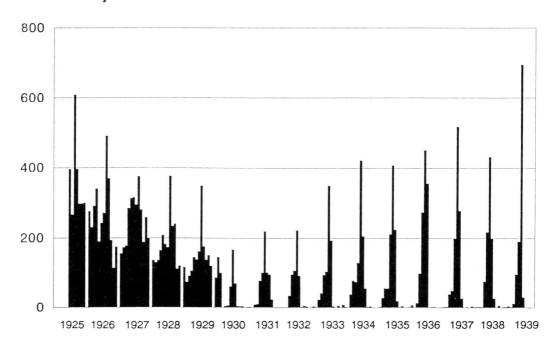

100. After passenger services ceased, down slate trains were braked by a locomotive, and ran only thrice weekly in the final years. An England engine passes the goods shed on 11th September 1941, the lake below it being Llyn Mair. This had been created to supply water for a mill and was later used in a hydro-electric scheme to give lighting to Plas Tanybwlch, the home of William Oakeley, a quarry owner. It had a private halt, one mile down the line from the station, and at one time the FR conveyed sea water there for residents to bathe in. (H.Wakeman/A.Gray coll.)

Workmans tickets

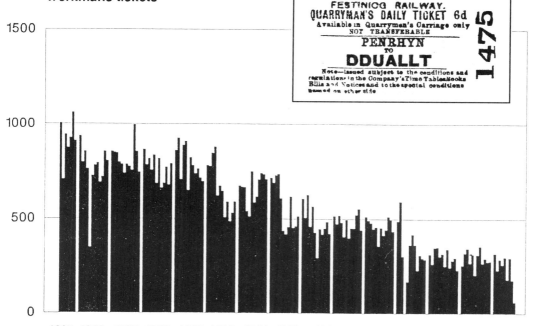

EAST OF TANYBWLCH

101. Above Tanybwlch the route is more than 400ft above sea level. The vistas of the Vale of Ffestiniog are memorable and were among the attractions promoted to the increasing number of tourists to North Wales. This indifferent picture shows neither *Merddin Emrys* nor the view at their best. Only the 60yd long Garnedd Tunnel occluded the scenic feast in this part of the grand concert. (FR coll.)

DDUALLT

102. This view of Rhosllyn (left) and the remote station is from an earlier era, as signalling was generally dispensed with when the FR received its Light Railway Order in 1923. In the 1930s this became a neglected halt although it was reputed to have once had a passing loop. It is here that the famous spiral line now commences.
(Gwynedd Archive Services)

103. An England engine emerges tender first from the south end of the 730yd long Moelwyn Tunnel on 11th September 1931. This inhospitable terrain was often difficult to work in the winter and the confined, very wet, smoky bore was unpopular with passengers and staff alike. In the background is Moel-yr-hydd and the slate producing district.
(L.V.S.Mann/FR coll.)

104. Lower right is the north portal of Moelwyn Tunnel and lower centre is Tunnel Cottage, built in about 1863 to house the tunnel telegraph instruments. Curving behind the cottage is the branch to Brooke's Quarry, double track in its first section. Granite chippings superseded syenite setts after WWI, large quantities being conveyed to Blaenau Ffestiniog and tipped into LMS wagons. The diverging trackbed (lower left) once led to a zinc mine, later used for slate production. This part of the route is now on the floor of Llyn

NORTH OF DDUALLT

Ystradau, the lower lake of the CEGB's pumped storage hydro-electric system.
(A.Gray coll.)

The following exchange of correspondence reveals Stephens' compassionate aspect and is reproduced with the original spelling and grammar.

To Stephens from Evans 21st January 1927

I have found out that Watchman R.Evans, Tunnel was not oiling the wagons that were coming from Brookes Quarry. I saw his wife and she stated that he is unable to do this work, and that, in fact, going into the tunnel affects him very much. I find that he is 78 years of age, and that owing to not being very well he is apt to drop in a faint. His wife admitted this to me this morning. I consider, he being in such a state, that he cannot carry out his duties about the Tunnel without being in danger of being hit or of falling down when trains are passing. She told me that they liked it at the Tunnel, but that she considers it is very lonely especially at night, should anything happen to one of them. They do not want to sever their connection with the Company, and she would like to know if we cannot give him a light job somewhere else on the Railway, and in the meantime she was asking if we could do something about oiling the wagons and also about going into the Tunnel, which, in fact, are the chief things that he is now doing. He has been with the Company for a period of 15 years, and has worked very long hours without any overtime for doing so. I shall be glad if you will kindly instruct me in the matter.

To Evans from Stephens 28 January 1927

I note what you say in your letter of the 21st instant. It is very unfortunate.

I do not like this old man, who has served us so well, being turned adrift, but I suppose he, and also his wife, will get the old age pension.

I do not like the pains in his stomach business. It looks as though he has got some trouble there.

See P.G.Pugh, how old is he, and see what you can fix up with him, and let me hear from you hereon, again, as early as possible. ("**please**" was a handwritten afterthought).

From Evans to Piercy at Duffws 21st April 1927

The funeral of the late R.Evans, Tunnel takes place at Penrhyn to-morrow. Will you please arrange the hearse is attached to the 12-55.p.m. down train to-morrow, Friday without fail.

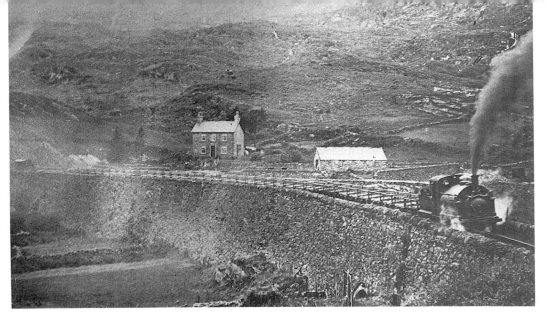

105. Approaching Tanygrisiau in about 1923 is an England engine with about 44 empty slate wagons. Sixty in a train was not an uncommon sight. A double engine had probably failed and so part of the train was left at Minffordd, a common source of annoyance to the quarry operators. The engine is near the site of the present exhibition centre for visitors to the power station and the cottage still stands, although the railway is now in a cutting behind it. The shed is at the foot of Wrysgan Incline. (FR coll.)

106. This site is now occupied by the road to the power station and is seen in 1940, as a barely discernible *Merddin Emrys* takes a load of slates down to Minffordd. They were packed tightly into the wagons to reduce breakages in transit. (A.E.Rimmer)

The letter below was sent to all members of staff on 2nd August 1946:

There will be no further traffic conveyed over this Railway and the service of the staff is dispensed with. I therefore regret having to inform you that your service will not be required after tomorrow the 3rd instant.
Yours faithfully,

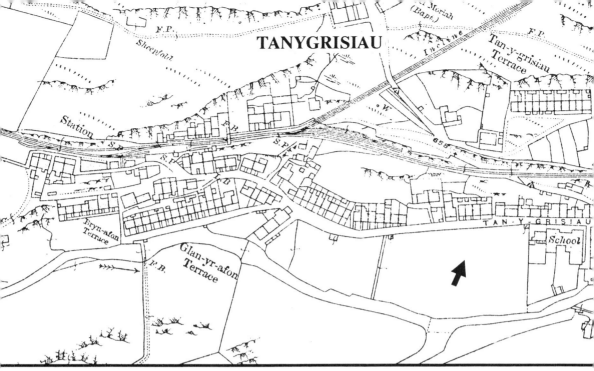

TANYGRISIAU

For over half a mile, the line is again on a shelf cut into sheer rock face, but in this vicinity there are rows of small houses in close proximity. These gave rise to considerable local traffic until the advent of a parallel bus service to Blaenau Ffestiniog. The incline (top right) was to the Cwm Orthin slate mine, a massive venture once employing over 500 men.

Ordinary tickets

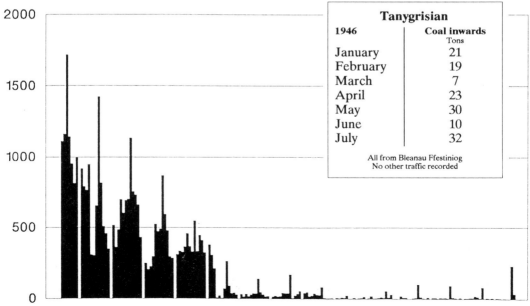

Tanygrisian	
1946	Coal inwards
	Tons
January	21
February	19
March	7
April	23
May	30
June	10
July	32

All from Bleanau Ffestiniog
No other traffic recorded

107.   Viewed shortly after closure, the extent of the buildings reflects the importance of this station in earlier years - it was enlarged when rebuilt in 1879. In its final years trains stopped by request only, and the points at the far end of the loop were removed. About half a mile north of the station a trailing branch curved eastwards to the Groby Granite Quarry, another source of chippings in large quantities for conveyance to the LMS sidings. (R.K.Cope/R.S.Carpenter)

Tanygrisiau 25th March 1925
12 loaded wagons derailed by a faulty flange.
Wagons severely damaged. Line blocked 10-0am to 13.30pm. Repairs to houses £32.10.6d. Payment to Maenofferen Quarry. Payment to Oakeley Quarry £137.10.7d.

Workmans tickets

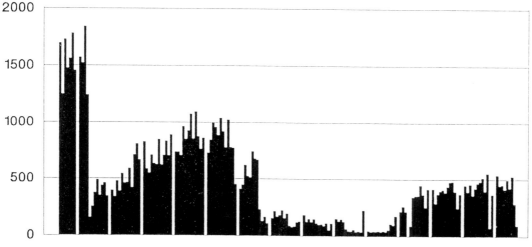

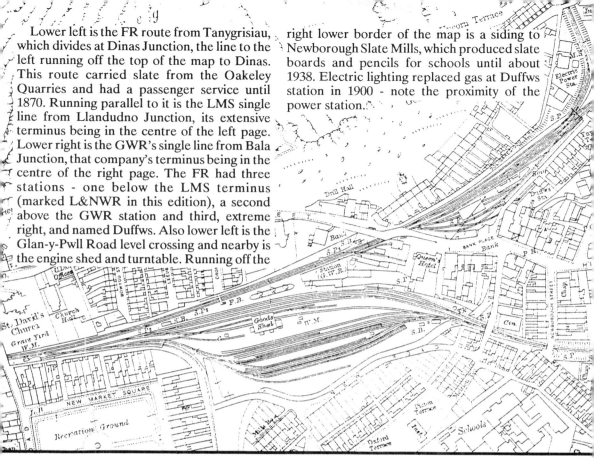

Lower left is the FR route from Tanygrisiau, which divides at Dinas Junction, the line to the left running off the top of the map to Dinas. This route carried slate from the Oakeley Quarries and had a passenger service until 1870. Running parallel to it is the LMS single line from Llandudno Junction, its extensive terminus being in the centre of the left page. Lower right is the GWR's single line from Bala Junction, that company's terminus being in the centre of the right page. The FR had three stations - one below the LMS terminus (marked L&NWR in this edition), a second above the GWR station and third, extreme right, and named Duffws. Also lower left is the Glan-y-Pwll Road level crossing and nearby is the engine shed and turntable. Running off the right lower border of the map is a siding to Newborough Slate Mills, which produced slate boards and pencils for schools until about 1938. Electric lighting replaced gas at Duffws station in 1900 - note the proximity of the power station.

LMS

←

108. A 1936 panorama shows (from left to right) the FR line from Tanygrisiau (with people obstructing it); the FR platform canopy, North Western Road; the LMS engine and carriage sheds; the ramped approach to the LMS station (in the centre of the picture); assorted LMS stock and an incline from Dinas up to the Oakeley Quarry. This station was burnt down in 1951, rebuilt in 1956 and closed in 1982, when the present one on the former GWR site came into use. (S.W.Baker)

109. With the LMS station in the background, *Taliesin* departs for Portmadoc with the now familiar train formation of the era. The parallel track was reserved for up mineral trains. Prior to about 1931 the two tracks between Dinas Junction and Duffws were allocated to passenger and mineral traffic separately, both running bidirectionally. (A.Gray coll.)

110.   This station opened with the adjacent LNWR terminus in 1881. The massive platform canopy was unique on the FR and was of great value as the annual rainfall here is several times greater than at Portmadoc. The enclosed area is endorsed *REFRESHMENTS*. The station was the last to be built by the FR. In the foreground is a loop that was formed from part of the mineral line until 1932. (A.Gray coll.)

Ordinary tickets

17th February 1928. No water at Blaenau Ffestiniog due burst water main ... water pumped from river ... later the river burst its banks ... blocked the line and stopped the shunting.

15000														
10000														
5000														
0														
	1925	1926	1927	1928	1929	1930	1931	1932	1933	1934	1935	1936	1937	1938	1939

111.　A closer view of the water tank seen in the background of the previous picture includes the ground frame. The school on the left was attended by children from Penrhyndeudraeth who travelled by FR. Letters from the headmaster survive, these complaining of late running of the trains and their effect on classes. (G.H.Platt)

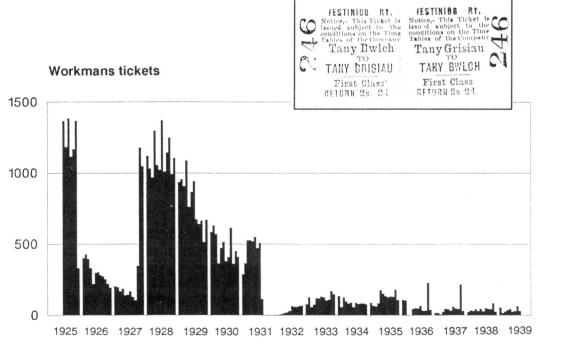

Workmans tickets

112. The LMS goods shed contained a narrow gauge track used for transhipment purposes. The ramped dock (centre) was used for the transfer of granite chippings to main line wagons, the other sidings being used principally for slate transfer. The photograph was taken on 14th August 1939. (Robin Butterell)

113. Looking from the LMS passenger platform seen on the left of the previous picture (but ten years earlier), we see a line of wagons and a brake van on the ramp. Above the letter "G" is a wagon in the tippler, which shot the chippings into the standard gauge trucks. (Dr. J.R.Hollick/A.Gray coll.)

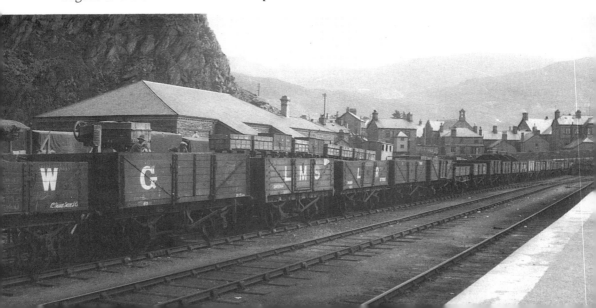

114.   Seen in the early 1920s, *Welsh Pony* is coupled to a slate wagon boarded for granite conveyance. The next wagon seems to be derailed. This part of the FR, through to Duffws, did not close in 1946 with the rest of the railway but, leased to the quarries, remained in use for slate traffic until 3rd November 1962. (K.Nunn/LCGB)

BLAENAU FFESTINIOG
GWR

115.   The LMS station is just beyond the Dorvil Road bridge, visible in the distance, and under which there were only narrow gauge tracks. The footbridge linked the platforms (GWR left and FR right) with Cromwell Street. The GWR goods and transhipment shed is on the left of this July 1936 view. (S.W.Baker)

Festiniog Ry.
FOR CONDITIONS SEE BACK
CIRCULAR TOUR NO.13ª
L. M. & S. ISSUE
PORTMADOC TO
BLAENAU FESTINIOG
THIRD CLASS
404)   404(S)(CTR)12ª
BLAENAU FEST.

7 AUG 1934   000

FESTINIOG RAILWAY
NOTICE.— This Ticket is issued
subject to the conditions on the
Time Tables of the Company
DUFFWS.
TO
PORTMADOC
FIRST CLASS Fare 2s.0d.

6491

116. Two GWR locomotives are evident on the right, while on the left a FR train has just departed towards the terminus at Duffws. The engine will have arrived there, the two stations being separated only by Queen's Bridge which carried Church Street. Few stations could have been closer and few towns could have had five stations in such close proximity. The signal seen in picture 74 had been sited to the right of the FR brake van. (Lens of Sutton)

117. This eastward panorama of the exchange sidings emphasises the loss of traffic that the FR suffered when the GWR arrived in the town in 1883. The passenger station is beyond the left margin of the photograph, which is probably pre-1923 but the scene changed little. This is now the site of a school and the FR/BR station. (British Railways)

DUFFWS

118. Although slightly before the era covered by this book, this photograph from June 1920 shows the west elevation of the station building and the nameboard. The signals were removed in 1923. The station opened in January 1866, alternate trains terminating here and at Dinas until 1870. (K.Nunn/LCGB)

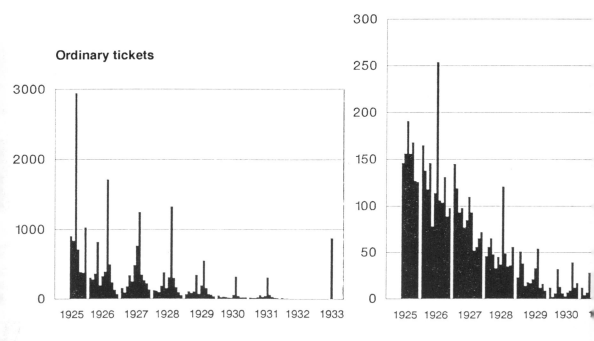

119. The station was closed from the first day of 1923 until the same day in 1925, except for quarrymens and goods trains. The goods shed was occupied by a builder from November 1929 and the station closed completely on 31st December 1931, after which date the lease was surrendered, but slate trains continued to run across the site until the end of 1962. Now the station building houses public toilets, a slate sculpture stands in place of the locomotive, the bridge has gone and the area is a carpark. (H.G.W.Household)

120. At the far end of the station a line curves left up to the Maenofferan Slate Quarry, where four miles of tramway over the hills linked other quarries to the FR. The incline in the background is to the Diphwys Casson and Votty & Bowydd Slate Quarry, which was taken over by Oakeley in 1933, the FR track conveying its output until production ceased in 1962. Thus there has always been some part of the FR in use since 1836. (British Rail)

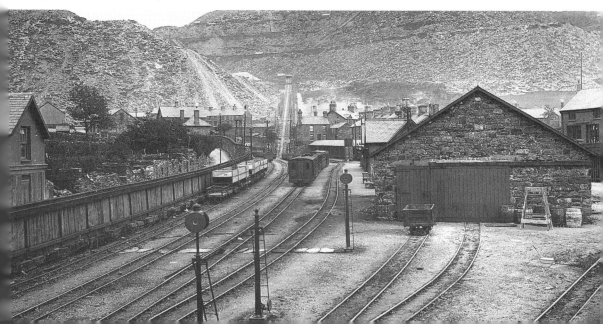